Contents

Introduction

What Meditation Demands of You

I don't need to tell you the physical and mental benefits of meditation. Plenty of people do that and, if you're reading this, you probably know them already. It's one of the best ways you can spend your time.

No, not spend.

Invest.

You earn that time back by being better, faster and calmer in everything else.

And yet, not everyone meditates regularly. Some people never try it. They have their reasons but, honestly, it's their lost. Then there are people who have attempted meditation and given it up.

Meditation is like exercise. You know you should do it and it makes you feel great. You still need to make it a habit, though. If something isn't a habit, it doesn't matter how simple or beneficial it is – it'll still take effort to do.

Or maybe you're one of the people who didn't get what you expected.

It's a strange thing to quiet your mind and draw your attention inwards. It's not easy if you're not used to it. Not thinking creates space in your mind for other thoughts. Maybe they're your normal thoughts. Maybe your brain starts shouting at you and throwing distractions. Or you might lose yourself in a daydream.

Meditation isn't about what you think (or don't think). It's a state of mind. While in a meditative state, you think in different patterns. Your usual perceptions and reactions go out the door as you explore a new mental frontier. If you find it hard to quiet your mind – if your mind even seems to fight you as you try – then I don't blame you for thinking that meditation isn't for you.

How many would-be meditators allow themselves to be discouraged by this? Probably most of them, based on conversations I've had.

If this is you, then that's okay. Take a moment to think about the reason you gave meditation a go in the first place. Whether you want to feel calm under pressure, reconnect with yourself, enhance your thinking or simply experience something new, let me tell you that you still can.

If you've struggled in the past, that's fine. Meditation doesn't demand a perfect performance. If you spend the session with racing thoughts... well, we've all been there. I've been meditating on and off for decades. I've spent over a year meditating every day. Even I struggle and yet I still get the benefits.

Your attitude is more important than your performance. Every session is a learning experience. If you can't concentrate, then you'll learn more than on the days you can. Be kind to yourself. Judging, analysing and criticising your mental state only shifts it away from what you want. Whether you are meditating easily in that moment or not, accept it.

Reality is perfect. You will get better over time, so acknowledge whatever is happening. Everything is fine.

And you don't even need perfection with this attitude. Some days you will judge yourself and that's okay. When you become aware of it, let the judgements go. You'll learn to let go of self-criticism faster and faster. One day, you'll be so fast that you never even think the thought in the first place.

Don't think that you aren't good enough to meditate. If you have a brain, you can do it. Your attitude is the main thing to focus on. Your abilities will increase in time.

Why Magic Isn't Real and How You Can Use It

I'm here to tell you that the old magics work. I don't believe in any fantasies. I'm a capital-C cynic who would point out that supernatural literally means 'not found in nature'.

None of this matters. Magic works.

How can I say that I'm a sceptic and I believe in magic? Don't be ridiculous. Magic isn't real and I never said that it is. I only said that it works.

What kind of magic? All kinds. Shamanism, Wiccan, Christian and D&D wizardry all work perfectly. You can use them to enhance your health, predict the future, banish problems, win battles and receive the wisdom of the gods.

See, the magic of magic isn't in some spirit realm. It lies in the rituals that people used to try (and fail) to invoke the blessings of pixies or whatever.

Magic isn't real but its rituals are powerful. Why? Because your unconscious mind loves rituals. This is why you have your little good luck charms and superstitions. This is how going to the doctor and receiving no treatment can still cure you.

Rituals and symbols are why you feel submissive (or hostile) around cops. They are why you have a certain style of dress, even if that style is 'I pick whatever so I don't have to think about it'. Going to your favourite park or turning on the TV after a long day are both rituals.

Everything you do can get the benefits of the most powerful spellbook, even as you obey physics to the letter.

People recommend having a dedicated place in your home for meditation. The idea is that you'll associate the place and the state together. Simply entering your meditation space will plunge you into a deep, pleasant trance.

Definitely do this. Then go even further.

The best magical rituals in fiction use ancient words of power. Choose your mantra and use it while meditating. Which ancient words of power? It doesn't matter! The words are irrelevant but the ritual matters to your inner mind.

What spell would be complete without great hand flourishes? Do whatever feels natural. Use huge sweeping movements or subtle caresses of the air.

Of course, the most powerful spells require you to have the right state of mind. No grump ever cast a Patronus charm. Find a state of mind that works for you.

None of these antics will do anything. At least, not at first. Keep them up and you'll associate them to the meditative state. When you do, you'll tap into the psychological principle behind every culture's ceremonies, chants, dances and festivals. Your inner mind loves rituals, so use them.

What Meditation Has To Do With Small Talk

I know of people who hate small talk. I get where they're coming from, even if I don't agree. Small talk is great. You realise this when you learn that small talk is not a simple exchange of information. Knowing what it really is helps you with your meditation practice.

Rituals are like catnip for your unconscious mind. If you want to meditate, then keep it happy. After all, your unconscious influences your attention and trance state. Meditation is little more than trying to meet your inner mind, so make it want to meet you.

The more a society moves their attention away from material concerns, the more rituals they create. Pay attention during a wedding (which is a ritual in itself) and notice how many smaller rituals they contain. If it's a religious service, you'll spot dozens of them. Every aspect of every religion overflows with precise, repeated sequences of events.

Churches often form tight-knit, supportive communities. The regular rituals play some role in this. The funny thing is that you get these results even with people who aren't religious. The ritual matters more than what it's about.

Even socialising has its rules and behaviours. Most of what you say and do with other people has nothing to do with either of you. When you ask how they are, you aren't asking a question. It's a greeting. If they gave an accurate answer about how they are, that's usually a faux pas. The correct answer is to smile, give a short response and return the question.

Talking about the weather might seem tedious if you think about information exchange. You both already know the weather and can learn more about it online. That's not what small talk is about, though. It's a ritual where two people suss each other out.

Imagine making a comment about how nice the weather has been. The other person smiles and agrees. That's pretty nice. It's a different feeling if they scoff, roll their eyes and point out that, actually, the weather has been awful, you idiot. The small talk has told you lot, just not about the weather.

Just like socialising and religion, meditation uses rituals of its own. When you close your eyes, get comfortable and draw your attention inwards, it's a precise and repeated set of instructions. Yes, these steps help you enter a meditative state, but they aren't essential. You can meditate with your eyes open and arms flailing if that's easier for you.

The existence of the ritual is more important than its contents. The part of your mind that creates meditative trances loves them. If you want, you can say a prayer to pixie folk as part of your meditation. It's wiser to ground your ritual in reality, though.

Set aside some time to meditate every day. Make it a habit (aka a ritual?) and stick to it. Use mantras if they help or ignore them. Begin by focusing outwards or inwards, but always in the same way. Your ritual might last a lifetime, so put a little thought into it.

When to Make and Break Meditation Rituals

How many of you dabbled with meditation and then quit? Even if you were getting benefits? I don't judge - it's easy to fall out of positive habits. Whether it's eating right, exercising, reading or delving into pleasant states of trance, life can distract you from your intentions.

This is why, if you're new to meditation, I recommend creating a meditation ritual.

Habits and rituals are similar creatures. Maybe a habit is showering and getting dressed each morning, whereas a ritual is more complex. If you ignore the surface flourishes, they both boil down to the same process. You perform predictable actions to get predictable results.

Your morning habits guarantee that you're dressed and smelling fresh when you leave. Your meditation rituals ensure that you easily enter a trance.

This is why most meditation coaches recommend that you set aside some space in your home. Only use this to meditate. Make it nice and comfortable. If you like mantras, think of a mantra. If you like music, choose some appropriate background tracks. This all becomes part of your ritual. Your inner mind sees that you're in your comfortable nook, listening to the right music and thinking the right thoughts, so it must be time to meditate.

It's great if you're starting out. I still recommend it even for more advanced meditators. But, if you truly want to take your inner skills to the next level, you should break your rituals. Meditate at strange times and places. Focus inwards while listening to loud noises or silence. Enter a trance using different mantras or none at all.

You know the benefits of meditation. It's one of the best things you can do, whether you want to improve your mood, resilience, physical health or enjoyment. Having a ritual is great because it makes you more likely to gain these benefits. Breaking the ritual helps you apply them to every part of your life.

If you can only meditate while in your designated spot... well, that's better than never doing it. Even better, though, is being able to enter that state at will. Anytime, anywhere. If work becomes stressful, you want to mindfully relax without having to leave your desk. If you are on a cruise ship halfway round the world, you want to still be able to enter a trance.

Meditation rituals are excellent springboards. They can become shackles, though. To truly integrate this practice into your life, learn how to create meditative states under any conditions.

Breath

The Best Way to Start Meditating

If someone tells you that meditation involves clearing your mind, it can be difficult to begin. How do you clear your mind, exactly? If, like most people, trying to think about nothing just leads to more thinking, then you can feel less than encouraged as soon as you begin. If you focus on something like the breath, however, your thoughts will more easily fade.

There's a reason why so many meditative practices involve your breathing. It's a strange thing. Unlike your heart rate, you can quickly and easily control your breath. If you don't consciously control it, though, your unconscious mind takes over and breaths for you.

You can think of your breathing – its rate and depth – as being the product of conscious and unconscious thinking. It's a bridge between two minds. Since meditation is all about relinquishing conscious control to your unconscious mind, it's a great place to start.

Even if you simply observe your breathing, you will learn more about yourself than most people do. Your body needs fresh, clean air – and more of it during a crisis. If you notice that you are gulping down oxygen, then your body is stressed. You might feel fine, probably because you've felt this way for a while, but you are burning yourself out.

If your breathing is slow, deep and steady, then it means you are relaxed. Your body isn't aiming for a quick hit but is instead making sure that each part of you receives the oxygen that it needs.

This process works both ways. Just as your state of mind influences your breathing, so does your breathing influence your state of mind. Don't think about its current rate or depth. If you want to relax and go into a meditative trance, then slow and deepen your breathing a little bit. Even a small change tells your inner mind that you are in a relaxed state.

Focusing on your breathing gives your mind something to do. If you are new to meditation (or even quite experienced) this will help. Thinking about nothing often leads to thinking about how you are thinking about nothing, which isn't helpful. But if you let your breath occupy your full attention, you can clear your thoughts and relax your body at the same time.

If you ever feel bored while paying attention to your breathing, then you're not really paying attention. Take a moment to breath in and out through your nose. Notice the feel of each inhale and exhale around your nostrils. Focus on the subtle differences with each cycle.

It doesn't take long before you are heading into a meditative state.

The Not-So-Secret Technique for Meditating Anywhere

Meditation is incredibly beneficial. It's some of the best training you can give your mind. It directly enhances your focus and mindfulness, which in turn improve everything from mood to memory. Any task that uses the brain (which is every task) benefits from regular meditation.

If you find it difficult to clear your mind, you're not alone. Don't use that as an excuse to give up though. Difficult things matter - they filter out the uncommitted, leaving only those with enough elf-discipline to continue. Be thankful that it's difficult, otherwise no one would appreciate it.

Don't use the difficulty as an excuse to struggle, though. Meditation involves clearing your mind. It does not involve stressing over whether you're clearing your mind well enough. All it requires is that you simply be.

This is why I recommend focusing on your breathing. It occupies your attention without inviting thinking. It brings your mind and body in sync. There's also the benefit of relaxing you. Simply pay attention to your breathing and it tends to slow and deepen. This puts you in a better state of mind for meditation.

And when you begin to realise how interesting, engaging and subtle your breathing can be, it changes the way you see the world. When your breathing fascinates you, there's nothing in this world that falls beneath your attention.

There's another benefit to training your mind using your breath. This benefit supercharges what meditation does for you. It deepens and enhances your practice, skipping over years of study (if you're dedicated, that is).

Are you ready for this secret?

I'm serious. This will sound simple but it's not. This will make the difference between you succeeding with your practice and giving up. If you take it to heart, you'll start reaping all of the benefits almost immediately. Anyone who ignores this will have to spend years working to catch up to everyone else.

Okay, the big secret is...

You can breathe anywhere. Your breath follows you.

Not impressed?

You should be.

When you learn how to use your breath to anchor your awareness, you can meditate in traffic. Or while talking with someone. Or while writing. If you want to bring a little calm, focus or mindfulness to any task, then you can use your breathing.

You can even use it while struggling to meditate. If your mind keeps wandering, then focusing on your breath will help you. It's the best way to recover from your mind wandering, whether you're meditating or living your normal life.

Let's talk about trance, baby

One of the problems with learning to meditate is that there are a lot of abstract ideas. It's hard to follow advice when it consists of things such as loosen your thoughts. How do you do that? What tells you whether it's working or not?

Two major hurdles that most practitioners face are not knowing what to do and not knowing if they've succeeded.

A meditative trance usually feels normal. If you're expecting otherworldly experiences from the start, you might get discouraged. That's assuming you can even follow an instruction as vague as 'release your attachment'.

Have you experienced either obstacle? If so, keep reading. I'm about to share a simple exercise that is measurable and puts you into a meditative trance.

When you focus on your breathing, your attention draws inwards. If you don't enter a trance, then you've at least set the stage for it. In time, your meditation practice can consist of nothing but mindful breathing. When starting out, though, it helps to go beyond it.

The next step is to deepen your breathing. Use your diaphragm and the muscles around your core to steadily inhale and exhale. Aim to keep the flow of air continuous. Smoothly draw the air deep into your belly.

If you find it difficult to breath like this, then you probably have tension in your abdomen. Spend the next few weeks practising. Keep your posture good and your stomach relaxed as you breathe with your diaphragm.

For anyone used to gulping shallow breaths into their chest, this alone is worth the time. You'll think clearer and have more concentration than ever before. You'll simply feel better.

And there's more.

Once breathing like this is automatic to you, aim to slowly extend each breath. It should be easy to add a second to each inhale and exhale.

If you feel short of breath or tense, then trust me when I say that isn't the point of this exercise. Chances are that you're tense or trying to slow each breath by too much. Dial it back and relaxed. Slow your breathing in an easy way.

This might take practice. If so, then take the time. The slower you build up, the faster you'll reach an optimal breathing rate.

What is the best rate of breathing?

About five to eight seconds to inhale, then the same time to exhale.

If you can breathe at this rate, deeply and in a relaxed way, then that's great. If not, it's something to aim for. Because if you can breathe this slowly and steadily without straining yourself and without feeling low on air...

... then you're almost certainly in a meditative trance.

Your breathing and mind are linked. If one is this calm, steady and relaxed, then so will the other be.

Body

Don't Lose Yourself in Meditation

The meditative trance is a wonderful experience. It should be part of your daily routine, if it isn't already. It opens yourself to new parts of your mind. Your thoughts and your body align and come under your conscious control. You cannot meditate too much.

Except... well...

Sometimes you can go deeper than you're ready. There's nothing wrong with this, of course. If you're one of those people who worry about being stuck in trance, you can relax. Anything that happens, you can reverse. In fact, often the trick is in keeping the changes.

But deep meditation can feel disorientating. It's a strange experience that might by physical. In this case, it's usually a form of dizziness.

It can also be mental. When this happens, you might not know where your mind is blank or not. That's shocking the first time it happens.

As I say, these experiences are fine. There's no danger beyond some mild disorientation. Honestly, a good movie should carry a similar warning.

Still, you might not want this. You might be the sort of person who enjoys having stable consciousness at all times. You'll learn to let go of that but, for now, what can you do to prevent losing yourself in trance?

There's a great meditation technique called the body scan. Everyone should learn it. Whenever you're feeling too caught in abstract nonsense and want to get real again, this is perfect. And you'll uncover more uses as you get better at it.

To conduct a body scan, place your attention at your head and move it down through your body. When you reach your feet, move your attention up through your body to your head.

It sounds simple but there's a lot to it.

If you're new to meditation, this is a great way to occupy your mind without thinking. Your body teems with sensory information that you mostly ignore. If you didn't, it would overwhelm you. Still, it's not healthy to ignore what your body is saying for too long. You might be surprised as you reacquaint yourself with yourself.

As your skills develop, it's a great way to tune your focus. You can place your attention on smaller areas. You might experiment with the depth and intensity of your focus. Maybe you'll see how slow you can move your awareness while still keeping your attention stable.

No matter what your skill level, the body scan is a great way to anchor your attention in reality. Your thoughts can seduce you but your body is real. Listen to it and you'll never lose yourself again.

Ultimate Focus and Awareness

There's a state of mind that sounds corny but is absolutely sublime. Colours are richer, sounds fascinate you and you can sense the air as it caresses every part of your skin. When people talk to you, you hear everything that they say and don't say. It'd be overwhelming if it weren't so pleasant.

Have a few moments like this and you'll never doubt meditation's benefits again.

It's a state of hyperconnectivity and hyperawareness. Reality floods your mind in slow motion. You feel everything, which sometimes means you miss the big stuff. That's only because you're tuned in to the tiny things you used to ignore. In time, you learn to integrate the two together.

That's where the magic lies.

If you're confused, that's my fault. It's hard to properly describe this experience. A much better approach is to experience it yourself. It's a great state to be in. Everything seems new, fresh and interesting. A bug crawling across a leaf is captivating while hedonism becomes quaint and irritating.

You should enter this state. I'm struggling to tell you why, so I'll move onto how.

Your body floods your mind with information. One of the roles of your unconscious mind is to block and monitor this stream. This is why you don't feel the shirt on your back but if an ant bites you, you feel it immediately. Anything important or predictable demotes itself to your background awareness. Your conscious mind is then free to focus where it chooses.

The first step to hyperawareness of the environment is awareness of the self.

You can focus on individual parts of your body. Pay attention to your hands or your lower back. Notice everything this part of you tells you. If you're new to meditation, this is a nice warmup.

Then you can expand your awareness to cover more of your body. The key is to avoid straining yourself. How much can you notice while remaining relaxed in your mind?

You can increase your coverage by practising this over time. The more you focus on large parts of your body, the more you'll absorb each time. If you want to speed this up, alternate between broad areas of focus and focusing on a single part of your body.

In time, your awareness grows to encompass your entire body. Some people find this easy while others take months of training to reach this. Whatever is right for you is right for you.

Once you get to this stage, or at least close to it, shift the exercise. Instead of seeing how much of you your attention captures, see how long you can hold this awareness. Noticing your entire body takes a lot of mental energy, focus and discipline. It takes even more when you keep your attitude calm, relaxed and accepting.

Hold your awareness for as long as is comfortable.

The aftermath of this state is indescribable. I tried to capture it in words and struggled. All I can say is that, if you can become aware of your entire body, noticing your environment becomes trivial.

Bully Yourself into Better Meditation

Meditation doesn't work unless you are kind to yourself. Many would-be practitioners go astray because they're mean to themselves. They judge. Nothing they do is good enough. They're failing at something. Comments like these have no place in your inner dialogue at the best of times. It's doubly true when delving into your unconscious mind.

But there is one technique from the art of bullying that makes your meditation smoother and easier. In fact, if you apply this in your life, it resolves pain and even makes you a better negotiator.

Ignore your parents and teachers with this one, because it's the ancient art of name-calling.

Labelling is powerful. There's a reason why schoolyard bullies resort to name-calling. It captures a lot of malice and condemnation in a nice little package.

I don't recommend doing that to anyone, especially yourself.

But when you label things with a neutral mindset, rather than a malicious one...

Well, I'm a big fan of taking tools of evil and using them for good.

During your meditation, you might notice discomfort in your body. Maybe this discomfort was always there and you're now noticing it. Then again, maybe it's from how you're sitting. If adjusting your posture helps, then don't wait for my permission to do so. Physical comfort matters a lot when meditating.

If it doesn't go away after a quick shift or a little wriggle, though, then you resort to name-calling. Friendly name-calling, of course.

With a calm, unjudging and neutral mind, label the sensation. If it feels like a prickle, simply think 'prickle' towards it. If it's a burning, try that instead. Don't worry about accuracy or precision - your attitude is much more important than picking the right label. If you want to keep it simple, use one of three labels: comfort, neutral or discomfort. Anything in your body is going to be one of those.

You might observe the sensation for a moment longer. Or perhaps you'd rather move on straight away. Either way, don't dwell on it. You've labelled it, so move on.

This works with physical pain, so long as your attitude is truly benign and accepting. It also works with social pain. If someone objects to your offer, label it in a calm way. "You seem concerned about our prices", delivered with genuine calm, is more effective than any amount of pleading, bargaining or backpedalling.

Bully your distractions with kindness and they'll leave you alone. Guaranteed.

The Lazy Way to Find Joy, Courage and Motivation

Everyone wants more of the good things. Happiness, love, charisma, success – which is your desire? Maybe you chose all of them.

Don't worry, I'm not about to tell you of the evils of desire. If you meditation long enough, you'll either discover that truth for yourself or you won't. Either way, me telling you isn't going to help things. Instead, I'll tell you something much better.

Those things that you want more of?

Meditation will help.

You'll unlock greater energy, creativity, serenity and anything else you decide to want. Best of all, it's easy. It's as easy as closing your eyes.

Now, when I say 'easy', that assumes that you're meditating regularly. That part takes discipline. Keep it up because here comes yet another benefit of the practice.

When you scan your body with your awareness, you surprise yourself. Your body hums with billions of signals that you consciously ignore. If you paid attention to everything, all the time, it would be a little overwhelming. With training, you can increase what you pay attention to, but there's always something that vanishes from your awareness.

If you haven't surprised yourself yet, give it time. Your body is a hive of fascinating activity.

As you scan your body, you find a few areas of discomfort and a few neutral regions. When you turn your attention in an accepting and perhaps forgiving way, the discomfort eases. Labelling the discomfort in a non-judgemental way soothes it too.

And neutral sensations often give way to other experiences. Perhaps what felt neutral was really a chaotic and intriguing blend of comfort and discomfort. Or maybe it was masking something new, something harder to classify.

What if the sensation is a pleasant one, though?

Well, the same rules apply. Observe it and accept it. Don't rejoice in finding something comfortable, as this condemns the rest of you. But maybe you can allow a brief glimmer of satisfaction.

And if you're looking for something in particular – joy or courage or whatever – then see if any is present here.

Be calm as you examine your sensations. You're not a kid tearing apart his room as he looks for his favourite toy. You're more like a swimmer trying to enter a lake without creating ripples. Use a soft touch – your thoughts are delicate.

Whatever sensation you want more of exists somewhere in your mind. If it didn't, you couldn't imagine it well enough to know you want it. And any sensation in the mind also exists somewhere in the body. So, with patience and finesse, explore your body and find it.

There are two ways to become stronger in this technique. One is to search without thought and effort. If you don't find anything, there's no disappointment because you didn't lose or fail. If you find it, there's no crowing over your triumph. The other approach is to look for what you seek in discomfort too. Perhaps your joy lies buried under a thin layer of unpleasant sensations.

You won't know until you look.

Senses

Access Your Inner Mind by Ignoring It

Most meditation coaches (myself included) will tell you to direct your attention inwards. But here's the thing - where's the fun in doing the same thing each time? There are no wrong approaches in meditation, only those that are less likely to work. So why don't we try to do the opposite of what everyone recommends?

If you struggle with meditation, then listen closely. The opposite of common wisdom might be exactly what you need.

I'm being a little dramatic. There are meditation coaches who recommend this technique. What I find interesting is that it's more common in the self-hypnosis community. Most things that work for one, work for the other, but the two groups don't share notes as often as they should.

When you combine the best techniques from self-hypnosis and meditation, you access your mind in a whole new way.

What is this technique that's the opposite of what most coaches teach?

Instead of focusing inwards on yourself, focus outwards.

Choose vision or hearing. Place your attention here. Use your mind to discern the shape and pattern of everything you're aware of. Focus on everything you see or hear. Open your mind, lower your defences and let the information pour in.

Once you lose yourself in the outer world, it's as if you lose yourself in your inner world.

And the best part?

You can meditate with your eyes open. You can do it while walking around. Heck - though I don't recommend this - you can do it while driving. The environment is rich, so drink it in and lose yourself among it.

Enter a trance by really seeing colour. Journey into your mind by following specific sounds. Let your consciousness dissolve as you gaze up at the clouds.

In other words, ignore your mind and you will enter it.

This process goes some way towards countering a common concern. Some hard-core meditators disengage from the world. The outer world can no longer compete with their inner experience, so they withdraw.

It's a shame and a waste. A good conversation with an experience meditator can literally change your life. The more you explore your mind, the more you see things differently. And what could be more valuable than a new perspective?

Paying attention to your surroundings, as a way of entering the meditative state, ties the two together. You can enter a trance and experience the world at the same time. And, in fact, you should.

Wean Yourself Off Reality

If you want to enter a meditative state, you can do it quickly and suddenly. If you know how to do that, then you can probably skip the rest of this article. This is for the rest of us. It's a technique to draw your attention inwards, even when your monkey mind is chittering out of control.

It's a simple matter of weaning yourself off reality. It's like easing into a warm bath, only the bath is your normal state of mind and you're easing yourself out of it.

The meditative trance state is strange and unusual. And so very normal at the same time. It's difficult to describe - partly because it's so different each time, partly because words don't cut it. A common experience, though, is experiencing the present moment without the usual mental clutter. It's either like seeing the world for what it is or what it isn't.

When familiar things - the sight of grass, for example - seem exotic to you, is that because you're seeing it for the first time? Or that you're mind sees something else?

It's not always easy to say. It sure feels like your slipping from reality - your normal reality, at least. And it's a pleasant sensation, even though it might not sound like one.

Does every trance come with a twisted view of familiar things? Not at all, but if you are experiencing this, you're definitely in a trance.

Which brings us to the technique.

If you experience everything as you always do, you may or may not be in a trance. So if everything seems usual and reality is in its place, then focus on one of your senses. Isolate them from each other.

A great way is to close your eyes and focus on the sounds around you.

Or maybe you'd prefer to pay attention to your sense of touch.

Your brain is very good at stitching your senses together. It knows that the orange thing, the hot thing and the crackling thing are all the same object - a campfire. Thank goodness, as without this you'd struggle to navigate the world.

But it's okay to switch it off for a while. Focus on one sense and one sense only. Stay connected to the outside world as you wean yourself slowly off it.

Your senses may feel strange when you dedicate your entire mind to them. That's okay - that's how you know it's working.

Disengage and Go Inside

Sometimes the world is too much. Crowded shopping centres, traffic jams and incessant thefts of your attention assault you every moment. And sometimes the world is not right. A few obvious changes would make everything better. So what can you do but disengage?

I love people but I don't like being in a crowd. They contain so much energy – adventure, success, connection – but they are hardly soothing. It's hard for me to find focus and serenity.

Or, at least, it used to be.

Even if you avoid crowds, the world is a busy place. You can't always escape the commotion, no matter where you live.

Sometimes you just have to let go to find some piece of mind.

Now, I don't recommend disconnecting from the world permanently. Some advanced meditators make that mistake. Instead of being overwhelmed by their environment, they allow their inner mind to consume them. There's nothing wrong with developing a mental state so enticing that the world doesn't compete. Just come back every now and then.

And let go every now and then.

The human brain constructs the past and the future with the same hardware. Memories and imagination come from the same place. Most meditation rightly focuses on what's real and what's present. The best meditators, though, can go the other way too.

Your senses ground you to the present. To be mindful is to observe what is happening. But your senses are simply another construct. It's almost the same thing to lose yourself in your senses as it is to lose yourself in a daydream.

Use your senses, by all means. Pay attention to your here and now. And know how to let go of it.

Your senses are signals. These signals come from your environment but they aren't your environment. Your brain is like a painter, reconstructing on canvas what they hear through a static-riddled radio.

Does that sound like it's worth hanging on to?

It is. Until it distracts you.

When you trust your unconscious mind, it's easy to hand over control to it. Let it monitor your environment for you – after all, it's already doing that. Let your conscious mind go. Ignore the signals and let them fade.

They say that reality is whatever remains when you stop believing in it. That makes money and love unreal, and they're both worth having. See what remains of yourself when you remove all that's real.

You might just surprise yourself.

Thoughts

Slow is Smooth and Smooth is Meditative

One of the many, many hurdles on the meditation path is speed. People want to rush things. They want results now. They want to enter an altered state of consciousness now. Hurry it up with the inner peace, would you?

Here's the truth: you don't get results by rushing. The only way to succeed is to take it slow. I mean that it takes time to build up your skills. No one is great at turning their attention in on itself in an instant.

I also mean something else by that remark.

You can think about meditation at the macro level. You develop this ability through skilful practice. This process takes time, no question.

Just like any other talent.

It's also true at the micro level, in the moment.

If you can't clear your mind of thoughts, that's okay. Here's a technique for meditating anyway.

What's the difference between the mind of a monk and the mind of your typical, cubicle-dwelling office worker? The one in the robes is in a state of perfect calm, stillness and tranquillity. The corporate drone is balancing a million thoughts. Some are related to work and office politics, others are not.

Really consider it. What's the difference?

Suppose a thought does enter the monk's mind. Is it the same kind of thought that floats through the corporate lackey's mind?

No. You're probably realising that the monk's thought is slower.

What does it mean for a thought to be slow? Think about your own thinking. A lot of it comes in loops. Maybe you have an unfulfilled dream that makes you unhappy, which makes you want the dream even more. Maybe you're simply noticing something that reminds you of something else, which makes you notice even more of the first thing.

A slow thought is one that moves through the loop slower. You become more conscious of the nature of the loop and how one thought leads to another.

Another way to think about it is having a song stuck in your head. Your thoughts will synchronise to the tempo of the music. If the music slows down, so do the rate of your thoughts.

By the way, this literally happens to me. Any song in my head tends to slow down so much it will become unrecognisable.

How do you do this? I'll give you a hint: if you start to think "yes! It's working! Look how slow those thoughts are going! Amazing!" then you're doing it wrong. All of your thoughts have to slow down, including those that observe other thoughts.

It's like taking energy out of the system. Everything calms and settles.

The Most Difficult Task within Meditation

Meditation is a complex artform. It consists of skills within skills and challenges within challenges. All of them are valuable, as they train your mind to function in a smoother, more effective way.

One important task is probably the most difficult. Everyone comes from different histories and personalities, so maybe you find this easier than others do. Having said that, most of you will struggle with this at first.

It isn't holding your attention stable.

It isn't quieting your mind in a relaxed, easy way.

What is it? It's nothing short of accepting your thoughts without judgement.

Judging your own experience is human. It's even useful – I won't deny that. But most, if not all of your suffering comes from this place.

At some point in your childhood, you experienced a series of sensations. Someone said you looked angry (and to cut it out and cheer up). In that moment, your young mind labelled a sensation as anger, and accepted a judgement of it.

This happened throughout your life. Sensations paired themselves to labels and judgements because that's what society told you.

There are cultures where anger is seen as a character flaw and others where it's a sign of a strong spirit.

You might not think this labelling and judgement applies to everything. After all, babies cry at the slightest discomfort, let alone pain. Surely we can agree that pain is a bad thing.

Maybe. And yet how you respond to pain changes how it feels. As Buddhism teaches us:

Pain is inevitable. Suffering is optional.

Don't believe me? The entire S&M culture thinks very differently about pain. They experience the sensation and then judge it in their own way.

This is what's so challenging about this. We're used to judging, labelling and assessing our experience. Is this ache worth checking out? Am I hungry or just tired? What would make this meal even better?

It's hard enough to suspend judgement on physical things. Thoughts are abstract. Separating them from your judgements is not easy.

This is worth it, though. Imagine losing all of the negativity around an experience. No one is freer than someone who genuinely loves their prison.

What's the technique for accepting your own thoughts?

Radical acceptance.

Whatever floats through your mind is good, proper and perfect.

When meditating, you don't want a tumble of distracting thoughts, but you don't violently suppress your thinking. As always, you release your thoughts in a calm and gentle way.

Do this while you're accepting your thoughts for what they are and you'll unlock incredible wisdom.

7 Words That Lead to Deeper Meditation (and a Happier Life)

There's a secret mantra, exchanged in dark halls, old monasteries and the quiet corners of the internet. This simple set of words isn't magic but it might as well be. Saying them to yourself transforms your mental state for the better.

If you're in meditation, this short sentence will take you even deeper inside.

Or if you're just walking around, it releases emotions and thoughts.

Write this mantra down and practice it. This exercise is one of the best upgrades to your mind.

Are you ready?

If your monkey mind won't stop chattering, then the mantra is:

"It seems that this body is thinking."

If you are blocked by an emotion, then your words of power are:

"It seems that this body feels angry/sad/tired/whatever."

These may sound simple. That's because they are simple and incredibly sophisticated. Any trained hypnotists or experienced meditators can spot the techniques immediately. For everyone else, let me break it down.

The first two words break any judgement. This is not the time for analysis or criticism. It softens what comes next by allowing it to be true or false.

After all, you're only describing what it seems like.

"It's cold outside" is a definitive statement. It's clear and without flexibility. Maybe it's not cold outside, in which case you'd be wrong.

And if you don't like the cold, that's a judgement. If you do like the cold, that's still a judgement.

Whereas "it seems as though it's cold outside" cannot be true or false. It's an honest description of what's going through your mind. It softens the statement, which softens any judgements within it.

This is important for what comes next.

Talking about "this body" is a classic dissociation technique. A common piece of sloppy thinking is when people say "I am angry" or "I am happy". This language sets up your identity. I am human, I am Australian and I am happy. That last bit is a different species to the other two.

No emotion is who you are. Your feelings are chemical reactions that you experience. They exist inside you and are part of your reality, but they are not who you are.

You feel emotions but you aren't them.

Identifying too closely with thoughts or feelings only gives them power. They make excellent servants and terrible masters.

The final part of the mantra labels what's happening. By this time, that experience has been stripped of judgement and dissociated. Adding a label gives your mind some way of identifying it.

I mentioned that these two mantras (and their infinite variations) take practice. The skill is not in the words themselves but in the mindset that would think them. Be the sort of person who naturally dissociates from their problems. Free yourself from your own judgements. If you do, you'll find your problems decide to leave you alone.

Emotion

The Danger with Meditation (and How to Avoid It)

There's something that most meditation coaches know but few will tell you. I'm not sure what motivates them to keep it to themselves. Maybe they think it tarnishes the meditation brand. Perhaps they don't know how to deal with it. I'm sure a few of them see it as "part of the experience."

This problem is certainly not a beautiful part of the process. It's easily manageable. And if you don't handle it properly, it can undo all the benefits you gained from meditation.

And then some.

So, what's the danger in meditating?

Most regular meditators reach a point where negative emotions bubble up. These could be anxiety, depression, anger or any other sensation that most people would label 'bad.'

It goes against meditation's brand. If you expect nothing but inner peace and euphoria, you will not see this coming.

And come it shall. Sooner or later, your brain vomits something that's difficult to handle.

Now, this can be one of two things.

The first possibility is that it's the mental equivalent of growing pains. I recently spent nine days with my mind constantly stretching, twisting and expanding.

For the first week, I loved it. I was happier and more excited than I'd been in a while.

At around the eighth day, I hit a wall. I felt frustrated at everyone and everything. Even though I knew what was happening and that it was irrational, there it was.

I wanted to tell everyone to go away… and not in such polite terms.

And yet, I was beaming at people. Not just smiling - beaming. My face was expressing genuine, heart-felt joy.

Part of me thought I was frustrated. The other part knew I was thrilled. Over a day or two, the frustration melted and the enthusiasm took over again.

This is what can happen when your mind expands. The walls in your mind move back and you can see a lot more than you're used to. It takes a bit to adjust.

The second cause of negative emotions needs more than just time to process.

Your unconscious mind keeps a lot of things from you. What you consciously experience is only a fraction of a fraction of a percent of what goes on in your mind.

Meditation brings unconscious material into conscious awareness. Most of this will be pleasant, useful or just strange. Some of it will be buried negativity.

Now, the good news is that, if your unconscious mind unearths something, then you're ready to process it and move on.

But if you're not expecting this, it can catch you by surprise. And in surprise is when we often make our mistakes.

You should do whatever you need to process this emotion. Most people should continue meditating; others might need a different approach.

Either way, how you proceed is important. What happens next decides how well you transcend the experience.

There's a saying in the hypnotist community: where attention goes, energy flows. In other words, if you fixate on something, more of your mental energy goes towards it.

So if you experienced anxiety last time, so you search your mind for anxiety, wondering if the anxiety is still there...

Well, that's putting all of your attention on anxiety.

If your boat has a hole in it, that's a problem. You need to pay attention to that. But your mind is not a boat and emotions aren't problems.

You should focus on what you want, not what you don't.

After what feels like a setback, use your next meditation session to focus on growth. Or serenity, or transcending your old limitations. Give your unconscious mind something to pursue.

Do this and you'll find that meditation lives up to the hype.

Using Meditation to Add, Not Remove

When looking at emotions, you can treat them the same way you treat thoughts. You can accept them, dissociate from them or let them pass.

But what if you don't want to let go of old emotions? What if you want to add something new?

Something better?

Mindfulness meditation is great for clearing out the garbage in your mind. Strange as it sounds, it's a tool of destruction. It clears the way for other things to blossom.

There is a tool of creation within meditation, though.

Something powerful enough to block the garbage in the first place.

People who master this technique are... different. I'm not one of them (yet - I'm working on it) but you can spot them from across the room. They are intense, in a warm and loving way. When they speak, every word seems loaded with wisdom and benign energy.

I mentioned that I'm still working on this. That's because I can reach this state, but I still have to turn it on. And that's not easy for me (yet...)

But when this is on...

Everything looks different.

Everything becomes better.

It's like looking at the world as it should be and seeing a way to bring it into being.

You can reach this state through meditation.

But not through mindfulness meditation.

This takes metta meditation, also known as loving-kindness.

Metta meditation trains you to see everyone the way you see people you love. This sounds simple because it is. It's not easy, though, as it goes against a very human instinct. Our ancestors had to be very good at separating friend from foe.

This instinct will probably keep you alive if you live in competing tribes. In a civilisation, it keeps you trapped.

Yes, there are people who mean you harm. Yes, there are thieves and worse who stalk the mean streets of this world.

You can love them anyway. After all, it must be terrible for them to view the world this way. I wonder how many of them could be redeemed with a single drop of loving-kindness?

Whether you hate or dismiss these people does little to them but a lot to you. Hatred, as the quote goes, is like drinking poison and expecting the other to die. So put away your anger. Do it for yourself, if not for them.

If you see this as weakness, then you don't understand it. This is the ultimate strength. To love strangers and enemies the way you love your friends requires a mind like iron. Developing this makes you impervious to anything they say or do.

Everyone has petty dramas in their life. If you want to transcend these, you now know how.

Should You Combine Meditation Techniques?

With mindfulness meditation, you have choices. You can focus on breathing, your body, your thoughts, your emotions, your senses...

Basically, you can choose anything and focus on that. As long as you are present and free from judgement, it'll work.

It's like having a buffet for the mind. Should you sample from each of them, loading up your plate until it groans under the weight? Or should you focus on one appealing dish and forget the rest?

I suppose it depends on what you're trying to do.

If you are new to meditation, then the main thing is to develop your skills. Holding your attention for longer and longer periods is your main exercise.

If you want a rock-solid foundation, then pick something to focus on and do not move on. Let's say you choose to pay attention to your breathing. You could spend a day, week, month or lifetime of regular meditating, focusing on nothing but each inhale and exhale.

Then, to keep your mind fresh, you switch to focusing on your body's sensations.

This robust protocol develops your skills. If you want to get good at meditation - and I mean really good - you need to master these basics.

But...

Well, what if you don't want to be a world champion at meditation? What if you're just looking for a little extra calmness, focus and tranquillity?

Then I'd say throw out the protocol and do whatever seems natural.

If you can hold your attention steady throughout your meditation session, then do so.

But if you're having one of those days where it's hard to focus, then switching what you focus on helps. Each time you move your attention, it's like a mental reset.

And the cool thing is that, yes, mindfully switching your attention may be easier for most beginners. It also happens to be great exercise later on.

Being able to move your awareness from your breath to your thoughts to your hearing, without losing focus, can be challenging in its own strange ways.

Or you might find it easier.

My philosophy is that any meditation is better than none, so do whatever works for you. Challenge yourself every now and then, but the main thing is to do it.

As a final thought:

For shorter sessions, it's easier to focus on one thing. For longer sessions, it's easier to switch between points of attention. Experiment and see what works for you. Some days you'll want a challenge; others, you'll just need to get through the exercise.

But in my experience, you get the best results by learning how to sustain your focus, then learning how to switch it.

Troubleshooting

How to Truly Let Go in Meditation

If you struggle with meditation, there's a good chance that this advice will help you. I'm not much of a gambler but I'd put money on it. It's something that every meditator experiences and, for many of them, it's their last experience.

Meditation is like anything else: some days are easier than others. Sure, some of you are naturals. And, yes, if your practice, it does become easier. But no matter how much experience you have, there are days where your thoughts loop and you can't let go.

It's tough. I know how bad it is - thanks to my obsessive personality, I'm probably poorly suited for meditation. It's something I've had to tame, channel and overcome.

This is good news for you.

Partly because my obsession with writing is why you're reading these words in the first place. And also because I know how to settle your thoughts, even when they won't cooperate.

It's a simple enough process. It's not easy, but it sure is simple.

To let go of your thoughts, emotions or whatever else is swirling in your head, then you need to start with this:

Stop judging yourself.

Now, this is a challenge at the best of times. Noticing that your thoughts are racing is a judgement. To settle your mind, I recommend practicing the art of noticing without judging. It's passive but don't let that fool you. It's harder and more nuanced than doing anything.

View your thoughts. Breathe through them. Know that whatever they are doing is good, right and proper. Accept them for what they are. And if your attitude of acceptance isn't perfect, then accept that too. This is the challenge - to avoid judging your thoughts, then avoid judging your judgement.

Another strategy is to bring your awareness to the present moment. This might make it easier to accept your thoughts, or accepting your thoughts might make this easier.

Your thoughts never race about the present moment. You either fixate on a memory or a projection into the future. Imagination and recall are both seductive, and meditation is the art of letting go.

You breathe in the present moment, so focus on that. You experience your body in the present too. Bring your awareness to anything that grounds you in now.

The final strategy is to give it time. Your thoughts probably won't settle immediately. Practice non-judgement and present awareness, and your thoughts will calm a little. This is progress worth acknowledging. Keep it up and you'll finally let go.

As I said, these skills aren't easy. You could spend years truly mastering them. Fortunately, any improvement in these yields results. As long as you keep working on yourself, you'll grow stronger.

Post-Meditation Gibberish Means It's Working

Now, this is not a universal experience.

It's pretty common. It happens to me all the time and I see it in others, too.

Some of you will read this and nod your head. For everyone else, keep this in the back of your mind. You might find it useful one day.

There's a curious phenomenon with meditation. You might go so far as to call it a side effect.

This phenomenon is where, after a really good meditation session, you suddenly become completely inarticulate. You can barely string two words together. I'm not talking about if you try to describe your session, you find your experiences don't translate well to words.

No – this is where you can't talk about anything.

Something as simple as your dinner plans leaves you grasping for the right vocabulary.

Like I say, not everyone will know what I'm talking about. Some lifelong meditators never experience it.

This is for the rest of us.

The best remedy for this is time. Your words will return to you. Simply take a breath or five. Your brain needs to switch gears again, then it will know what to say.

If you don't have time or you don't want to wait, how can you speed this up?

It helps to know what causes it.

The brain has two hemispheres – left and right. It's a misconception to say that you favour one or the other. All complex tasks use both hemispheres. But it's also a misconception to conclude that they are the same. Each specialises in different styles of thinking and logic.

Your left brain tends to be more analytical, its thoughts are more linear and it likes to think of the past or future. The right hemisphere tends to be more open, parallel and thinks in the present moment.

This is an oversimplification, of course. Your brain is complicated and no simple model can capture it. Even so, it's pretty accurate.

Language mostly comes from the left hemisphere. But notice that the right one pays attention to the present moment. When you practice mindfulness meditation, your right brain temporarily activates more than your left brain.

The better you held your attention on the present, the more intense this imbalance becomes.

Of course, this shift is tiny. It's not like your left hemisphere switches off and you become a blubbering, irrational goofball. But if you find yourself unable to find the words, it's because that part of your brain has put its feet up and it enjoying a rest.

Time restores your balance. If you want to speed it up, then start engaging your left brain. Count from one to ten, then start over. Pay attention to specific details in your environment. Make it clear in your mind where your body ends and the world out there begins.

And, of course, you can practice speaking. That's the surest way to find your words again. It's also a good measure of how far deep inside yourself you went and how quickly you're returning.

Instead of Ignoring Distractions...

One of the big challenges with meditating is learning to handle distractions. It shocks no one to learn that it's a useful life skill, too. Staying focused despite noise, discomfort or even your own thoughts will transform more than your inner life.

It's a challenge. No one will pretend that it isn't. Some days your thoughts are calm like a pleasant stream. Other days the world around you is a turbulent mess.

Good meditators can enter the right state no matter where they are. Let me tell you from experience that being able to meditate on international flights is amazing.

Great meditators can even handle their thoughts being noisy.

It's funny - even as I write this, I'm getting distracted. There are noises outside, which are nothing compared to the ideas popping into my mind.

That's okay, though, as I'm still writing. And my meditation sessions are similar.

In fact, the problem's worse when I'm meditating. When my mind is quiet, that's when ideas start flooding my mind.

At least, they try to.

The trick is not to ignore distractions. That takes effort and is itself a distraction. There's a much better way to keep you on task.

Suppose that your young child brings you a drawing of theirs. That's cute, right? But let's assume that this is the ninth drawing this hour... and, to be blunt, they're not very good.

What do you do? Do you yell at the child? Tell them to leave you alone? Pretend they don't exist?

Well, you could. It might even stop them distracting you.

But I hope it's clear that this is not the best approach.

What do you do? You take the picture, smile, thank them for the beautiful drawing and wonder if they can make an even better one.

It's a loving, accepting, patient attitude.

Strange as it sounds, it's often useful to treat your own mind like a child. If you are meditating and fixating on distractions, don't blot them out. Acknowledge the thought or sense, and thank your mind for bringing it to your attention. Calmly explain to yourself that you're busy right now. Later, you can give any distractions they have your full attention.

Now, though, you need to focus on this.

Meditation is the ultimate me-time. You need to protect it, even from yourself.

But it can never be a clash of wills. When you fight your own mind, you lose no matter what. Calmly owning what you are entitled to is the smarter way to win.

Meditate the Way You Enter a Hot Bath

Some days, meditating is easy. Other days is seems impossible. If you're starting out, maybe every day feels like one over the other. As you become more familiar with the techniques, there are more of the good days.

It helps to know what to do when you're having a bad day, though. Maybe you're new to all of this or perhaps you've got a lot on your mind.

Life happens. You don't have to be perfect.

And thanks to one awesome technique, you barely even have to be decent.

The trick is to meditate the same way you'd enter a hot bath.

You know what I mean. You dip your toe in then recoil out immediately.

Then you go for it a second time and it doesn't seem as hard. Maybe you make it to your ankle before pulling out.

On the third try, you lower yourself in a few times.

Then you simply ease into the warm water and let it envelope you.

You can meditate this way, too. Just like with the bath, it's a lot slower but its success rate is phenomenal.

If you're trying to meditate and it's not working, that's okay.

Open your eyes. Breathe. Bring yourself back into your normal state of awareness.

Then go again.

Close your eyes, draw your attention inwards and do whatever meditation techniques you like.

And if it still doesn't work, repeat the cycle. Then repeat it again. Keep going until you're in a state of meditation.

There's a principle in hypnosis called fractionation. The idea is that bringing someone in and out of trance brings them deeper into trance. It's strange but it works. Each time they go back into trance, they go deeper and faster.

It's the same with meditation. Every time you close your eyes, it gets a little bit easier.

Think of it like a warmup. Runners stretch before exercising and this is the mental equivalent. The experience guides you to better results.

And let me tell you this:

This exercise builds your meditation skill like nothing else.

Reaching a state of meditation, even when you struggled with it, is like training with weights on. The difficult days are where you learn the most. The struggle is where you progress.

What I love about this is how friendly it is. If it's too challenging, then stop, take a break and start again. It's so effective and enjoyable that you have no excuse for not using it.

The Simple Exercise That Fixes Your Breathing and Posture

A key element in almost all meditation is your breathing. Another key element is your posture, although that's mostly because it affects your breathing. Getting these right goes a long way towards making your experiences comfortable and effective.

They are also great for the rest of your life. Breathing balances your mind and your posture balances your body. Whether you want power, stability or health, you really want balance.

Luckily, one exercise corrects both at once. Talk about value for your time.

I will warn that it involves lying on the floor. If you have back issues, look after yourself first. If you have young children or pets, maybe lock the door.

Lie on your back and look up at the ceiling. You can use a pillow to support your head if you need. Without a pillow, though, you'll gain a sense of how your spine feels when properly aligned.

Memorise how your posture feels. It should be as straight and relaxed as this while meditating.

I'll come back to your posture. Let's talk about your breathing now.

Place one hand on the centre of your chest. The other should go right below your belly button.

Then, while still on the floor, breathe. Inhale and exhale as naturally as you can and notice what your hands do.

Most people will notice both hands moving. Some people will realise that only their chest moves when they breathe.

If you want to be calmer, feel less stress and have more energy, chest-breathing is not your friend. You want to spend us much time breathing with your diaphragm as possible.

Especially while meditating.

Adjust your breathing so that your chest doesn't move. Your belly should inflate and deflate like a balloon. Keep your breathing slow, steady and comfortable.

Practice this. Ten minutes of this, three times a week, will even transform how your voice sounds when you speak.

Take it easy, though. If you ever feel short of breath, don't push through that. Listen to your body at all times.

When you get used to diaphragmatic breathing, the next step is to try it while standing. The act of standing engages muscles to fight gravity, so you'll find that it's harder. Your breath will want to rise to your chest because of tension in your abdomen.

Relax and breathe until your chest doesn't move. Not even a millimetre.

And you'll find, by no coincidence at all, that the only way to breathe with your diaphragm without feeling short of breath. You'll notice that when your breathing is perfect, so is your posture.

Maybe their favourite thing is playing with their children. Perhaps they love their jobs.

If you have activities that you love, then you can use these to meditate. If you often lose yourself in the activity - if it leaves you feeling recharged or at peace - then I have good news. That's the state of meditation.

You might think it strange that something like tennis can be meditative. After all, tennis is about speed, sweat and excursion. But how many tennis players experience time slowing down and the world going quiet, even as they move to intercept a 200 km/hr tennis ball...

Meditation isn't a special class of thinking that only happens in monasteries. You experience it all the time in your life. It's about harnessing, expanding and appreciating something that you already do.

The next time you meditate, keep that experience in the back of your mind. Anything that brings you closer to that state is good. If you move further away from it, go back to what you were doing before.

The Inner-Blocked

Then there are people who struggle to access their unconscious mind. Their emotions are dulled, their imagination is grounded and the descriptions about playing tennis made no sense to them.

There's no judgement here. If you think I'm describing psychopaths, I'm not. Some people live highly intellectual lives. There are thousands of rewarding careers that need people like this - people able to rationally think through a problem without getting distracted.

There's nothing wrong with pursuing satisfaction instead of happiness.

If you find meditation difficult because you're too conscious, this might be you. When someone tells you to close your eyes and go inside, you don't know what that means. It's an unclear instruction and, boy, that must be irritating.

You can learn to meditate anyway. The question you might ask is whether you should.

The general rule is that exploring your unconscious mind enriches your life. It adds unconscious material to your conscious awareness, which opens up what you can do. It gives you more options without detracting from anything you have.

Having said that, what you find might surprise you. Most people have a lifetime of experience dealing with strange unconscious materials. Things like random emotions, strange memories and unusual thoughts flicker through our minds all day. If you're not used to it, it can be unsettling.

My advice would be to find a meditation coach. Not just any coach, though. You'll want someone who understands where you are coming from.

Ideally, they'll have gone through the exact process too. They'll know how to guide you to the next step and how to handle anything that comes up.

Working with them might be the greatest decision you ever make.

Benefits of Meditation

Why this chapter is near the middle of the book, not the start

Most meditation guides give you a list of benefits up front. They talk about how meditation keeps you calm, centred, focused, healthy and a hundred other things.

I decided to go in a different direction. I wanted to talk about how to meditate before explaining why you should.

What drove me to buck this trend?

It's quite simple, really.

That list of benefits isn't real. I'm not saying it's a lie - you definitely experience them.

It's only that they are side effects from the true benefits.

Okay then, you ask, what are the true benefits?

...

... it's hard to say.

That sounds like I'm dodging the question. It's true though. It really is hard to articulate.

Imagine upgrading from on old, fuzzy, dying TV to a state of the art model. Everything looks so much clearer. Meditation is like that for the mind.

Some things that used to bother you lose their power. Your thoughts seem different, slicker and more aligned.

These words don't capture it. It's better than it sounds.

And by putting it towards the back of the book, there's a better chance that you know what I'm talking about.

You may have experienced this. Maybe you have a sense of what I mean, as if the true benefits are lurking just outside your awareness. It might be a vague intuition of the raw power of your own expanded consciousness.

If not, it will come.

But if you do have a sense of what I mean...

Keep going.

You already know that something amazing is coming.

Keep going.

How Genius is Like Stupidity

As you learn a skill and develop your abilities, there comes a middle point. From this point, the road before you looks an awful lot like the road behind you. In a way, mastery is a regression back to your baseline...

Novices see the world in a simple way. This is because the novice ignores most of the information in front of them. Think of someone learning to drive. Before they sit behind the wheel, they think it'll be easy. They've seen adults do it without any drama.

You just turn the steering wheel and go, right?

A master at driving also sees it as a simple task. They ignore most of the information, paying attention only to what matters.

Then they just turn the wheel and go.

In between these two phases - near the middle point - driving is complicated. There is so much information to pay attention to. Lanes, speed, other cars, your destination...

They turn the steering wheel while information floods into their mind.

Both geniuses and dunces see things as simple. The path to mastery is about learning complexity, then how to simplify it.

What separates the masters from the novices is focus. Novices don't know what to pay attention to, so they ignore almost everything. Masters also ignore almost everything, but they narrow in on the one relevant detail and decide from there.

This is the true power of strong focus. Yes, it keeps you on track. Yes, it allows you to ignore lesser priorities. But its real virtue is being the heart of mastery.

The better you can focus, the more able you are to fixate on the relevant details. Once you know what to focus on, mastery accelerates.

And the best way to train your focus is through meditation. If you can pay attention to your breathing, then you soon realise you interesting it can be. There are so many sensations involved in inhaling and exhaling. Until you notice them, every breath seems the same.

Like a novice ignoring all the details.

When you learn to find interesting variations in your breathing, you can apply that to anything. If air moving in your nostrils is interesting, people are fascinating. You'll never suffer through a boring conversation again, because you realise there's no such thing.

Monks can stare at a rock with rapt attention, mesmerised by its features and details. As the sun moves through the sky, it lights the stone in different ways. You can learn to see more of it through the power of focus.

And when your focus is this powerful, everything else in life becomes easy.

Applied Neuroscience Secrets of Ancient Mystics

The power of meditation is the power of your mind. It trains useful mental skills that lie at the heart of everything you do.

For example, focus.

Learn to do that and nothing won't become easier.

For example...

If you want techniques that improve your memory, the best place to turn to is the latest neuroscience research.

The second best place is a book by William Walker Atkinson.

Memory: How to Develop, Train and Use It is over a hundred years old. It is remarkably timeless, though. Not everything that he wrote still holds true... but most of it does.

A hundred years ago, they knew a lot less about how the brain works. You'd be surprised by how much they knew about using it, though. Atkinson drew on the techniques and traditions of ancient cultures.

And many ancient cultures knew a lot about maximising their memory.

Before the printing press, books were written by hand. If you owned a library, it meant you were rich. If you were lucky enough to be literate, the best most people could hope for is to borrow books.

And if you have to give books back after a week or so...

Well, you'd better memorise as much as possible. Otherwise, you're just wasting your time.

That's not even mentioning cultures that memorise their holy texts. These people need to be word-perfect with long, complex writings.

You can't do that without solid memory skills.

So the brain may have been a black box to them. But they sure knew how to wield it.

The arts of memory require dedicated training in a range of techniques. But there's one principle that you need to master before you can even begin:

You can't make a good copy of a bad recording.

If you're not paying attention, then it doesn't matter how good your memory is. If you walk through life in a mental haze, then you won't notice anything. And if you don't notice something, you won't remember it.

Focus is important. It's the first step in all mental processes. If you don't pay attention to something, you won't remember it, learn it, appreciate it...

The list goes on.

Through meditation, you learn to still your mind and focus on what's in front of you. Master this and nothing else, and your memory will naturally improve. Your thoughts will organise themselves better around good copies of clear records.

And if you decide to learn memorisation techniques on top of that...

Well, who knows how far your memory will develop.

Breathing Under Pressure

What's the opposite of choking under pressure?

Breathing through it.

'Choking' is a metaphor, of course. When you get nervous or flustered, it's not like your airways close.

But they sometimes tighten a little...

In the moment, it can feel like you can't breathe.

The remedy for that is to breathe anyway. Take control of your breath cycle and your emotions will fall in line.

Here's a question, though:

What causes people to buckle under pressure? How is it that a superstar is flawless in practice but can make mistakes in a game? What makes it so hard to talk to a crowd, even though it's easy to talk to friends?

Well, the context is different. There's more at stake. There's pressure.

I get that.

But think about it for a moment:

Let's say you're meeting with a client. You know the facts and you're normally relaxed. And yet, as soon as you meet them, something inside you freezes.

Now imagine you meet with a client. You meet every question and objection with the right answer. You're smooth, calm and charismatic.

In other words, you're the real you.

What's the difference here?

Evolution is a merciless optimisation process. How could evolution lead to a species that's capable of greatness, except when the stakes are high?

It's almost as if your conscious mind knows what it wants, while something else inside you is confused...

What evolution created was a part of your mind that tracks social reality. Every person you see, it assessing them as friend or foe, threat or opportunity, rival or mate...

It also tracks your position in the social group. Some part of you knows whether you're the alpha of this group, the beta or somewhere further down the pecking order.

These roles shift constantly and you're always, on some level, aware.

Humans without tribes didn't survive long in our ancestral environment. Your ancestors needed to know what the group thought at every moment.

Meeting a client, giving a speech, playing sports when a thousand eyes watch you – these are unusual social contexts. The part of you that tracks your social rank doesn't know how to assess it, so gets concerned. If it doesn't know who the alpha is, it seems safer to stay in the middle of the pack.

This is why visualising your success is so powerful. It primes your mental state to assume you'll succeed and it calms this social tracking mechanism.

And in the moment, you can always focus on your breathing. Control what you can control to bring everything else in line.

If you want to improve both of these skills at once, learn to meditate. The entire art revolves around controlling your breathing, enriching your mental landscapes and soothing those parts outside your conscious awareness.

Meditation and Mental Health

If you want to live a more fulfilling and satisfying life, it pays to strengthen your mental health. The stronger the pillars of your mind are, the better able you are to live the life you truly want.

A healthy mind takes action, unhindered by fear, confusion or distractions. And it keeps working when things get tough.

Your mind is the product of your entire lifestyle (and, I suppose, the reverse is also true). Looking after it is like looking after your body. You'll want to live right, eat right and sleep right. Your mind needs social contact, interesting puzzles and physical movement to stay at its best.

Looking after yourself draws on every aspect of your life. So meditation is not the whole answer, though it's certainly part of it.

Q: How does meditation improve your mental health?

Firstly, nothing I say here should be construed as medical advice. Only a licenced professional who has, you know, spoken to you would be qualified for that.

But, for most people, meditation is great training for your mind's health. Just like physical exercise keeps your body strong, meditation develops key mental skills. Focusing on the present moment keeps you from dwelling on the past or worrying about the future. Accepting what you experience reduces the sting from any negative emotion.

You don't lift weights to get good at lifting weights. You do it to become strong in your everyday life. Meditation is the same.

Some quiet time also allows your unconscious mind to work through any issues behind the scenes. When you meditate long enough, you'll have days where you come out of it feeling great. You won't know what resolved, but you'll know something did.

That makes you stronger for whatever happens next.

Q: How much should I meditate each week?

If you've never started before, take it slow. Maybe you want 10 minutes a day, three days a week.

You want to build that up. Most people find it better (and easier) when they do 20 minutes every day. That's what I do, at least.

Then sometimes I will meditate twice in a day or have a longer session (about an hour).

Whether that's right for you is up to you. I encourage you to try longer sessions, though.

Q: Does meditation help with more serious mental health issues?

It can. There's a lot of evidence that meditation is great for things like anxiety, stress and trauma – even PTSD. For serious conditions, I recommend seeking guidance – at the minimum, talk to your doctor. You probably want a good meditation coach too.

Meditation generally isn't recommended for people who hallucinate or have split personalities.

Your body's mechanism for enhancing your health

There's a principle in medicine that applies to everyone. It doesn't matter whether you're healthy or not. It doesn't matter whether you have a genetic condition, an old injury, a nasty infection... or if you're in the prime of your life.

This principle underlies modern medicine and alternative medicine (at least, the ones that work). Every doctor and healer by other names knows this to be true.

It's the cause of more healing than anything else on the planet. It does contradictory things, like boost your immune system or restrain it, to improve your wellbeing.

And when you understand it, you can use to keep yourself safe, healthy and full of energy.

Are you ready to hear what it is?

In scientific terms, your body is amazing.

It is truly, genuinely amazing.

You're alive in a world full of things that can kill you. Injuries and infections lurk at every corner. And yet here you are.

Genetics have not changed much in the last 100,000 years. You have the same basic structure as your hunter-gatherer ancestors. They had to fight, hunt and forage for every scrap.

There were no tools except what they could make. There were no medicines except what they could gather.

In this world, they survived for decades. They laughed, wept, found love, raised families. Many of them lived full, rich lives in a world with rival tribes, terrible predators and diseases that could infect a simple scratch.

Their bodies - your body - kept them alive and well, against the odds.

Your body is amazing.

This is the principle: no medicine of any kind heals you. All it does is restore balance and remove obstacles enough for the body to heal itself.

Modern medicine knows this. The body does all the work - all doctors need to do is interfere occasionally to set it on the right track. There's nothing in a hospital that tells cells to repair a cut. Nothing, that is, except the patients.

Your body constantly heals itself. Every day, you wear yourself down. Every day, you build yourself back up. This balance can keep you alive and vibrant for decades.

But there's only so much energy to go around.

If you perceive a threat, you need to act now - maintenance can wait. If you put the wrong foods into your body, there's less of what the repair mechanisms need. Without sleep, rest and downtime, the balance tips away from health's favour.

Meditation gives your body time to do what it needs to.

It calms the system, freeing resources to go where they're needed.

Your mind strengthens, steering you towards better habits.

And it brings your awareness to what your body says it needs.

This is how meditation helps you stay healthy. It does little directly to fight off infections or repair damage. Indirectly, though, it liberates your precious resources from being squandered on the wrong things.

Your body and mind are a team. Teamwork best when both parties show up.

How I Dream Up New Ideas

Some people have accused me of being creative. It's a charge I won't bother to deny. After all, I write every day. You need a high volume of ideas to feel comfortable doing that.

But it's an awkward moment when someone asks how I think of so many topics to write about.

The truth is, I don't.

I don't think of them, that is.

They emerge like details in a dream. Do you know what I mean by that? In a dream, you can walk around a house and the ceiling is blurry and patchy. Then you look up, and texture and lights add themselves to the scene. They aren't there until you pay attention to them.

That's how I come up with new ways to think about things. Those, in turn, give me what to write about.

I don't do anything. The only credit I can take is being aware enough to listen. There's a voice in my head - the ancients would call it my muse - that whispers new insights to me.

The best way I can hear the whisper is by quietening my mind.

Hold onto your hats, folks, because this is about to get meta.

Because that's how I came up with this article.

I wanted to write about how meditation opens your mind to new possibilities. Your conscious mind is analytical and precise. It's great at following recipes. When you need to deviate from a recipe - to think something new - that's where your unconscious mind comes in.

And a great way to bridge conscious and unconscious material is through meditation.

But how do I convey that?

Well, my muse whispered, with a story.

What kind of story?

How about my muse? It deserves a chance in the spotlight.

This is not my usual style of writing. And the topic - writing about writing - isn't something that I often deal with.

My intuitions are telling me to go for it, though. I can hear the call (and trust them) thanks to hours spent with a quiet mind.

If you have a mental block and need new ideas, meditation will help you.

It might take time and practice.

Then again, how might be a natural.

Either way, it's worth it. The meditative state opens you up to more possibilities than you can imagine.

I mean that literally. The ultimate idea machine lies obscured by the fog of your own awareness.

So pull back the curtain and use what is yours.

Beyond the Benefits

Meditation is a Terrible Way to Relax

The way most people come across meditation is they're looking for a way to relax. The problem is that it's not a relaxation technique. If you begin by expecting nothing but calm and comfort, you're in for a shock.

Is it relaxing?

Sure, usually.

Will it reduce your tendency to get stressed in the first place?

Definitely.

But so will reading, jogging, exercising, feeling gratitude…

Meditation works on deep levels of your mind. It expands your consciousness by bringing suppressed thoughts into your awareness. Unlike what Freudians will tell you, not everything that's suppressed is a bad thing. Expanding your consciousness gives you greater control over your thinking.

Relaxation is a side effect.

So if your main reason to meditate is to feel calmer, you'd better be prepared for the rest of it.

Now, I will say that not everyone will experience this. Some people meditate for years and only feel a light, pleasant relaxation. If that's all they want, then good for them.

But most meditators reach the stage where they break through to something new. It's like opening a door in your house that you never noticed and finding a ballroom on the other side.

This is wonderful. The only word that comes close, for me, is transcendence. A wave of new thoughts, memories, experiences and perspectives floods your mind.

It is sublime. This epiphany enriches every corner of your mind.

This is why I started meditating in the first place. I kept running into barriers in my life. A major one in my teenage years was that I was irritable, even angry.

Every day, some trivial experience would get under my skin and make me lash out. (Verbally.)

I didn't like who I was, so I turned to meditation.

Thank goodness I did, because it expanded what I was capable of. In every moment, I had choice. Yes, I could get angry. Or I could feel happy or calm. The options were mine.

This is transcendence – realising that there's an easy way around the problems in your mind.

Most of your problems disappear when you stop doing X and start doing Y. That's easier to say then do… until you expand what your consciousness is capable of.

But if you're meditating to relax and suddenly your mind blooms...

Well, it freaks some people out. Not because it's bad but because it's intense and unexpected.

They just wanted to chill out – they never signed on for becoming enlightened.

If this happens to you, you have two options:

Stop meditating. If you want to relax, take up knitting or something.

Or keep meditating. Take care and take it slow as you integrate these new avenues into your mind.

One feels good. The other is like gaining superpowers.

The Peter Parker Moment

Anyone who knows me knows that I love superheroes. Sure, they're tacky, cheesy and predictable. Those are just reasons, though, and since when do people like stuff because it's logical?

Superhero stories speak to us because there are so many drivers woven in to them. There's something for you there, whether you like adventure, power, the nobility of fighting for what's right, the ultimate celebrity status they enjoy…

Or maybe you like watching people come to terms with something greater than themselves. Their life changes in a moment. Everything they thought was possible is now completely out the window.

They have to live their normal lives while carrying this much potential inside them.

If you meditate long enough, you know what I mean. There's a sudden leap in your consciousness. Things that used to stop you now seem laughably trivial. Things you used to take for granted, you now deeply appreciate.

And no one around you notices.

(At first…)

What kind of superhero does this make you?

Superman was born exceptional. He grew up with godlike abilities coursing through his bloodstream. His rise as a hero was deciding how to use those powers – for good, or for evil?

Then there's Batman, who dedicated his life towards a single purpose. He focused all his resources to his mission of ridding Gotham of crime.

A hero like Iron Man is a different take on it. He had the ability to build his suit all along, but he never realised it. It wasn't until he was backed into a corner and fighting for his life did he have the breakthrough.

And then there's Spider-man.

Peter Parker didn't want superpowers. He wasn't expecting them. At no time did he plot, scheme or experiment to gain them.

He didn't choose where or when to gain his powers. He didn't choose what his powers would be.

One moment, he was "just" Peter…

The next…

Some people see meditation as more like Bruce Wayne. After all, you put the work in over a long time to get results. Or maybe more like Tony Stark, who spend a life preparing for the one epiphany he needed to transform.

I don't disagree with those perspectives. They're no doubt true for many people.

My experience is more like a Peter Parker moment.

After disciplined meditation, something suddenly awoke. I didn't choose where or when. I didn't choose the form of my new thoughts.

But they were exactly what I needed.

Now, not all of these new perspectives were useful to me. Unlike superheroes, we have the luxury of ignoring what powers we don't like.

This frees us to pay attention to the ones we do.

I'll admit that it's not a perfect metaphor. For example, only one radioactive spider bit Peter, whereas you will have many of these breakthrough moments.

And the more you have, the more you'll be able to shape them. You can choose your outcomes and design your mind, like Tony Stark.

This makes meditation better than getting superpowers. With this analogy, it's like getting all the superpowers you want… as long as you put in the time.

Crouching Coward, Hidden Shadows

There comes a time in your meditation practice where something seems to awaken inside of you. This powerful experience can literally change the way you see the world.

Some people suddenly become more perceptive, more intuitive and better at business.

Others release emotions they've held for decades.

And there are those who have stranger experiences still.

It can happen in an instant. It can build up over weeks or months. Either way, it rips apart your old thinking the way a baby chick rips apart its shell.

Suddenly, there's a whole new world to explore.

The only thing left is for you to figure out how to navigate it. It's lucky that you've trained in the best techniques to do that.

Here's what not to do:

In *Crouching Tiger, Hidden Dragon*, the main character -Mu Bai - runs away from his monastery. He was deep in meditation when he reached a state of pure emptiness. This void was not the bliss of nirvana but just a crushing, hollow sensation.

It scared him, so he ran.

Now, I get it. I've glimpsed a sensation like this from a distance. It's never consumed me like it did him, but I understand the urge to run away.

But the part that confuses me is that he did run away. Not that he had the urge but that he acted on it.

He found something dark within his mind and he fled from it.

Me? I would have endured it. Mu Bai, being an actual monk, would know more of meditation than I do. Even so, I know enough to know how to breathe through emotions. To accept them, no matter how challenging. To persist without thought, analysis or judgement.

Am I really claiming to be wiser and braver than a fictional warrior monk? That seems unlikely but the results are what they are.

I doubt I'm stronger but maybe I have more faith in my unconscious mind.

It's common for meditators to experience strong - almost overwhelming - negativity. Whether it's a void like Mu Bai's, or anger, sadness or grief, it happens.

Something that your unconscious has held on to, and hidden from you, steps out from the shadows and into the light.

Why?

Why would your unconscious mind wait until you meditate to release it?

The answer's simple:

Because it knows you're ready to face it.

Your unconscious mind shields you from a lot. That's one of its duties in your mind. It doesn't like to suppress anything, because then it lingers, but it's better than releasing it when you're not ready.

If you experience it, then you're ready.

Be brave enough to accept the challenge.

You can choose to run from it, to suppress it again, to let it rampage through your consciousness. That teaches your unconscious not to trust you with important matters.

If you stay present with it, knowing with conviction that you can handle this, then the trust placed in you pays off. You resolve something that's been lurking in the shadows for a long time. Once it goes, you can live a life that's beyond anything this limitation could keep you from.

Work through this as you have worked through everything else in your meditation practice. Seek help if you need it. But know that your mind never gives you a challenging emotion that you can't handle.

Unconscious Psychology

The Part of You That's Everything Else

If you're doing any sort of deep work with your mind - meditation, hypnosis, psychotherapy, shamanic rituals, whatever - then you're changing at an unconscious level.

But you might wonder what exactly the unconscious mind is?

It's pretty simple, really.

There's your conscious mind. That's everything you're away of.

The unconscious mind is the part of you that's everything else.

Now that we've cleared that up...

Okay, okay. It's not a great explanation. Let's see if we can do better.

A part of you regulates your body functions. It tells your heart to keep beating, your body to remain at a certain temperature and your muscle to fire in precise sequences. You can't control these processes consciously. You aren't even aware of the thoughts that control them.

That's your unconscious mind.

Then there's the part of you that controls your emotions. Sure, you can consciously hijack this to an extent. Thinking of someone you love changes your emotions, for example. But you can't switch off (or on) sadness the way you can lift your arm.

Your emotions come from your unconscious.

You have automatic protection mechanisms. When you touch something hot, your hand recoils as if on its own. If a car speeds towards you, you leap out of the way without thinking. If something appears in front of your face, you blink to shield your eyes.

This is your unconscious.

There are skills and habits you once didn't know, like walking or driving a car. At first, you couldn't do it. Then you could do it but it took a lot of (conscious) attention. Then it became so automatic that you didn't have to think about it.

Once more, your unconscious at work.

These categories don't even begin to scratch the surface.

Have you ever tried to remember someone - a name, a fact - and "some part of you" forgot it anyway?

When you speak, do you choose each word and inflection?

When someone is angry, isn't it usually pretty obvious? But what part of you, I wonder, instinctively analyses the emotions of other people?

There is a lot that goes on outside your unconscious awareness. In fact, you're not aware of a thousandth of a percent of what you think and do.

It would overwhelm you.

Both in terms of volume and variety. The unconscious handles everything from basic biology to complex intuitions.

This is what makes meditation and other mental practices so powerful. It brings some of the unconscious material into your awareness.

And it teaches the rest what you want in life.

Why do you need to teach it? Shouldn't it know what you want, seeing as how it's part of you?

Honestly, I don't know. I'm not sure if anyone knows. Maybe it's a protection mechanism to keep us from things we think we want. Perhaps it's because, given the amount it processes, the unconscious mind doesn't know what to focus on.

All I know is that mind training helps. It will surprise you, if you let it.

How to Program Your Autopilot

Thinking is harder than you think.

If you've ever spent a day stretching your mind and running new thoughts, then you might have a hint as to what I mean. It's exhausting in a different way from exercising your body.

But like physical exercise, working beyond your limits is a great way to remove them.

When you grow your mind like this, it takes a lot of energy. Food, water and sleep are (usually) essential. I say usually, because everyone responds differently. I tend to sleep less and eat a lot more after intensive thinking.

It takes a solid chunk of self-care, too. When you're outside your normal thought patterns, old memories and buried emotions can surface. This is a good sign - a sign of growth. Even so, your mind can have growing pains just as your body does.

But what makes this the case?

Our brains evolved for adaptability. Shouldn't our minds thrive with new thinking?

Well, they do. But thinking our usual thoughts is always easier than thinking new ones.

You can imagine someone born into a hunter-gatherer tribe. As a child, they had to learn a lot. In fact, they had to learn everything.

The entire world was new to them.

As they grew into adulthood, their models of the world stabilised. Sure, there were always changes. Night is different from day; summer is different from winter. New tribes out there and new members in their own tribe shifted the political balances.

These shifts, though, were within tight parameters. They were tweaks to the world, not reinventions of it.

This is why habits work. Yes, even in today's world where "change is happening faster than ever before." Habits save you time and energy by responding in predictable ways.

By the time you're a teenager, let alone an adult, you have a complex web of habits. It takes focus and willpower to break these routines. Even in your own mind, certain thoughts trigger specific reactions.

Change takes more effort than remaining the same. After all, your brain assumes that most things won't change. Fish won't replace birds in the sky and rocks won't turn into ice cream.

Your habits keep your life stable.

But sometimes that's not what you want.

Sometimes that's not what you need.

In that strange state of mind that meditation and hypnosis create - the trance state - your mind is open to new possibilities. Your conscious mind likes to lock things down and keep them stable. It likes following habits, routines and procedures.

Your unconscious mind, though, seeks meaning out of chaos.

It likes to change.

It's happy to think new thoughts.

Yes, it still takes energy to think these. And it takes even more to decide whether these new thoughts are worth thinking...

But meditation is like switching off your habits. Your mind is free to think in new ways, develop new habits and discard the old ones.

It's nature's way of changing your mind.

Misinterpreting Reality as a Mental Shortcut

Our brains operate on strange (and strangely sensible) rules, especially at an unconscious level. These rules make sense when you sit down and think about them.

Then, when you think about them more, you realise that there are huge leaps of logic.

One of these rules is the Law of Association. It's a principle that your unconscious follows to efficiently add meaning to raw sensory input.

It's kept you and your ancestors safe, happy and alive.

And it works thanks to fallacies and hallucinations.

When the hallucinations stop being useful, it can be hard to escape the pattern. That's when practices like hypnosis and meditation help.

The Law of Association goes something like this:

A hunter-gatherer is out on a hunt. They see a tiger stalk and kill an antelope or something.

Impressive, they think.

They just learned that this animal is a mighty predator. Useful information.

Then they cross into a tiger's hunting grounds. It ambushes them. They fight it off, thanks to luck, weapons and the advantage of numbers.

Terrifying, they think.

And rightly so. The tiger is capable of harming them. They should fear and admire it, just as they fear and admire all the greatest hunters.

But that's not what the brain does. It wants to prevent injury but it doesn't follow that chain of logic. It doesn't think: "that's a tiger, tigers have attacked humans in the past, it might injure me, and so I should fear it."

Your brain skips from "tiger" straight to "fear."

It associates the two concepts together.

Later, the hunter-gatherers learn that tigers like specific types of grass to hide it. Their brains associate that grass to tigers to fear.

Before long, they go straight from "grass" to "fear."

The fallacies are that the grass itself is safe. Not all grass hides tigers. Not all tigers are dangerous. And not all danger is scary.

The brain ignores all of that. It takes time to properly process the chain of associations. And you might make a mistake somewhere in that chain.

So the Law of Association compresses everything down. If a certain song reminds you of someone you love, hearing it is the same as seeing them.

If you love your job, entering your office is the same as doing the work.

When things correlate, your unconscious reasons, there must be an underlying cause.

Is that always true?

No.

But it generally pays to assume that it is.

So much of your reasoning about the world is hidden from you. Take the time to explore your logic – especially when it doesn't serve you.

The One Choice That Changes Everything

There's one principle from unconscious psychology that is beyond powerful. Even if this is the only thing you learn from me, you'll quickly grow happier, wealthier, more productive and healthier.

You can use this to correct minor foibles or completely overhaul your life.

And it works in any domain – whether you're an athlete, business professional or someone looking for love.

Do this and you'll start spotting opportunities. It'll feel like magic, as if the universe is responding to your desires. These chances were always there but, for the first time, you start to pay attention.

It all comes down to a choice that anyone can make at any time.

The simplest and most powerful decision:

What do you choose to focus on right now?

Because in unconscious psychology, the Law of Attention says that whatever you focus on is what you get more of.

Pay attention to the good things and you get more of them. Focus on the bad and... well, you can get more of that, too.

This isn't some empty philosophy telling you to "think positive!"

It's solid psychology telling you to pay attention, right now, to what's working.

There are people who choose to focus on the negative. They criticise everything and everyone. An hour in their presence can make you want to punch something. They poke holes in every idea and explain how every achievement is really a failure.

And the strange thing is that these people are miserable.

Shouldn't they be happy? After all, in their minds, everything around them is broken. This makes them the lone hero, the voice of reason.

It makes them better than everyone else.

But no, they are bitter and miserable.

That's because they actively seek out (or create) negativity, so they wind up with more of it.

They focus on the bad stuff, so more bad stuff happens.

Don't be this person.

Then there are the genuinely joyful.

They see beauty and opportunity everywhere.

I'm not talking about being naïve or overly saccharine. When bad stuff happens, they accept it. But they choose to focus elsewhere.

In their mind, the world is full of amazing people doing great things. Isn't it humbling, even demoralising to live this way?

It turns out it's empowering. Focus on empowerment and that's what you get.

This choice you make with your conscious mind trains your unconscious. What you focus on teaches your mind what you want. If you pay attention to your successes in romance, then you'll follow opportunities to get more.

If you fixate on your failures, then it's time to rethink your mental strategy.

A practical strategy is to choose three times per day – morning, lunch and just before bed. Review your day and notice what worked. Pay attention to what you did right. If you made mistakes, then focus on what you can learn or what you did right within the mistake.

Do this until it becomes a habit.

Then follow the habit until it becomes your way of seeing the world.

When Your Body Shields You From Attacks

Meditation, hypnosis and similar practices bring your unconscious mind into your conscious awareness.

That's great, but what does it mean?

And who cares if unconscious material floats into your attention or not?

Those aren't simple questions. Your unconscious mind controls everything from automatic biological functions (breathing, heart rate, etc) through to complex instincts.

Including those instincts that keep you safe.

The more you listen to your inner mind, the better you can hear that intuition that keeps you out of harm.

I think about this whenever I remember something that happened to me years ago. This isn't the nicest story so, if you're squeamish about violence, then consider averting your eyes.

I was riding a crowded bus in the middle of the day. That's important - this was no darkened alley in the seedy part of town. This was in full sunshine with dozens of folk in spitting distance.

This guy had been riding the bus too. He had made neither peeps, fusses nor scenes. There was nothing remarkable about him. He was maybe on the scruffy side, but so what. I was a university student at the time - people probably thought that about me.

Anyway, for some reason he chose me out of everyone on the bus. He walked up and asked if I had any money. I said, truthfully, no.

And then my arm flew to my face...

... to block his hand that was lunging for my throat.

Now, I hadn't done any martial arts. No self-defence courses. Nothing like that. I don't know how I knew what he was about to do. I don't know how I knew what to do about it.

The great thing about instincts is that you don't have to know. All you need is to act on them.

Then I got lucky. The bus came to a sudden stop, so he released me to keep his balance. Then he hopped off the bus, turned around and started yelling at the driver. I say 'yelling' when it was more like...

Well, it doesn't matter. Everyone walked away in one piece.

The point is that my unconscious mind detected a threat and diffused it. Meanwhile, my conscious mind was scrambling to catch up. Had I had to think about it, I would have been far too slow.

Your unconscious mind scans your world for threats. One of the purposes of mind training is to teach it what threats are real and what you can release. If you have a phobia of dogs, then something inside registers a pampered poodle as a danger. Same with public speaking - it's something harmless that's considered a threat.

You can unlearn these.

When you train your mind, it frees you to be happier and safer.

Enhance Your Learning

We've always described the human brain with metaphors. It's too hard to describe it, you know, accurately.

Back in the day, people saw the brain as like being a vast, complex set of pipes and hydraulics.

Then the metaphor changed. As soon as telephone exchanges became popular, the brain was like them.

Then, of course, the famous "a brain is like a computer" comparison.

With the internet, we see a powerful, dynamic, ever-changing network. Finally an almost-decent comparison.

Because the brain is not a computer, set of circuits or bundle of pipes.

If it were something so mechanical, learning would be easy. After all, how does your computer learn a skill? You install new software and...

There is no 'and.' That's it.

With our wet, squishy brains, though, it's not that easy. You might want to learn something and struggle. Even if you don't struggle, it takes a lot longer to learn a skill than to program a computer.

It doesn't work as it should. Something as simple as remembering someone's name can elude you. Genius-level skills take decades of hard work.

And between those two extremes is everything else that can escape your attention.

This is because learning is not a conscious activity. It happens purely on an unconscious level. Some part of your inner mind decides what to learn and what to ignore.

It follows deep logic of its own - simply 'wanting' to learn something isn't enough to convince your unconscious.

Not by itself. The logic is complicated.

Everything you learn has to fit in with everything you already know. You don't just add a fact to your brain - that fact is assessed against every other fact, perspective and paradigm you have.

This is what stops you from learning the wrong things. Some things, like "the sky is solid" and "you owe me ten grand," don't gel with your version of reality.

But sometimes this mechanism gets it wrong. You'll probably ignore good advice that scares you, for example.

Unless you make a habit of engaging your unconscious mind.

With, say, meditation or hypnosis.

The trance state trains your mind (consciously and unconsciously) to be more open to new ideas. "Open" in a good way - you won't act against your interests, but you'll at least consider ideas before rejecting them.

And you'll fit them into your web of memories better.

Stories engage your unconscious mind, as do real experiences. Sitting in a classroom? Maybe, maybe not. Our ancestors never learned anything worth knowing through long, dull injections of information.

True learning experiences create their own trance states. The more you practice entering trance, the more easily this will happen for you.

The Language of Your Unconscious

When you meditate or experience hypnosis, you're more likely to hear when your unconscious speaks to you. This has to be experienced to be believed. If I list the benefits this brings to your life, there are two common reactions.

If you've never explored your own unconscious mind, you'd scoff in disbelief.

On the other hand, if you do have experience with this, you'd scoff at how incomplete my list is.

So I won't talk about the benefits you gain when you attune to your unconscious... except to say they're worth it.

When your inner mind starts speaking to you more, it can be confusing. Maybe even a little overwhelming.

But don't worry - your unconscious has been speaking to you in its language all your life. It may be a little louder now, but you're fluent.

What are you fluent in?

The language of symbolism.

A great example of this symbolism comes from the history of science. You might already know this story but, even if you do, really think about what it means.

This tells you so much about unconscious psychology:

August Kekulé was a 19th century chemist. One of the great challenges in chemistry at the time was benzene. Scientists had deduced the structure of many chemicals but benzene seemed to defy all logic.

He thought about the problem and all the confusing data benzene yielded. He had all the information he needed to solve it but his conscious mind couldn't find the answer.

Then, as the story goes, Kekulé fell asleep in his armchair. He had a dream of a snake eating its own tale.

When he woke up, he realised that benzene wasn't a chain like everyone thought, but it was a ring.

This isn't the only example from history of nap-fuelled epiphanies. Dali and Edison both used short naps to free their minds, showing it works in everything from art to engineering.

It's a testament to the problem-solving powers of your own unconscious.

But why use symbolism? Why didn't Kekulé's unconscious say, "yo, August, benzene is a ring, not a line"?

(Apart from him speaking German...)

All creatures with brains solve problems. Not all of them use language. So in the deepest structures of the human brain, those that evolved before language, lies a powerful well of creativity.

72

Besides, language (as we know it) isn't the only way to solve problems. If you label something, it becomes more real in your mind.

This is useful, don't get me wrong.

But sometimes you want to make things unreal.

When the answer is something you've never thought, limited thinking is the last thing you want.

This is why symbols are so powerful. A word might have one or two definitions, but a symbol can mean so many things.

Take a flower. It can represent beauty and love, of course. But can't a humble seed pushing through dirt represent determination? Or resourcefulness, potential or growth?

Some flowers are edible, so it could mean food to you.

(And food can represent energy, health, community, socialising, enjoyment, reward...)

Your unconscious mind works on all of these levels, and more, simultaneously. That's why you often get your best ideas when your conscious mind steps out of the picture. And it's why there's no such thing as empty symbolism.

Get Free Coaching from Celebrities and Dead People

There's a curious quirk with the human brain. It's how it's possible to navigate the social context without our heads melting.

Because think about it: in order to do just about anything, you need to predict how other people react.

But you can't simulate another brain (and maintain your own) without being orders of magnitude smarter than they are.

Somehow, you manage. Sure, it's not perfect, but you can usually predict how people will respond.

When to use flattery and when to be stern, for example.

This quirk of your unconscious mind can let you learn insights from people you've never even met.

Even people you could never meet.

The funny thing is that it even works with fictional characters.

It's all to do with how you think about other people.

People are complex black boxes. You can't pull them apart and study how they work. But you do have one important advantage when it comes to predicting them:

You're a human, too.

Don't underestimate its value. If you want to know how your friend Jim will respond to something, think about how you'd respond to it.

That's a pretty good approximation. He'd prefer $50 to a punch to the gut - you know this because you would, too.

But you can get a little more sophisticated.

For example, you know (from earlier observation) that Jim is prideful and impatient. So you wonder how you would react to something if you were prideful and impatient.

The amazing thing is that this works. You can imagine yourself having a different personality well enough to think as they think.

What's even more remarkable is how normal this is.

Yeah, everyone says, of course you can change your personality by pretending to. That's obvious.

Obvious? Yes and also miraculous. What incredible power lies in your unconscious mind!

This is how you can learn from people you've never met.

Think of someone - anyone - who you admire. It could be Elon Musk. It could be Julius Caesar. Or Sherlock Holmes. Living or dead, real or not, it doesn't matter.

Then wonder how they'd approach a given situation.

How would they talk to their friends and solve their problems? How would they think about things in your life?

Your prediction won't be perfect, but it will be strangely good.

Do this and keep practicing. Simulate the thought habits of people you admire. Keep going until you forget that you're pretending.

Then you have it:

Free coaching on demand from anyone. Anyone at all. Living or dead, real or fiction, you can picture how they think and thus learn from them.

How I Learned That I'm Not a Pile

Our minds do not view reality directly. We can't process most signals from our environment. Those we do go through a series of electrical and chemical transformations before they reach the brain. There, your mental software has to process it to make sense of it.

There may be light around you, but your brain never sees it. It infers its existence from raw data.

And if it did so faithfully, that would be one thing. But any neuroscientist or psychologist will tell you that we hallucinate our mental models into existing.

When you look at a banana, you don't see a banana. You see splotches of colour that match the 'banana' pattern in your mind. Without touching it, you assume it's soft and sweet. You don't assume it's rigid, scalding or a predator.

The biggest illusion that your brain creates is a tricky one to spot.

It makes you believe that there's a 'you' in your head.

It's like the riddle of sand. A single grain isn't a pile. Two grains next to each other don't make a pile. Three don't and four don't... but when you keep adding grains of sand, it eventually becomes a pile.

Likewise, a single thought doesn't make something a mind. Neither do two thoughts, or three.

Have enough thoughts and it sure feels like your sense of self is real.

In both cases, it's an illusion of labelling. Humans find it useful to distinguish a handful of grains and a pile. Reality herself makes no such distinction. The truth is that there are no piles or even grains. It's all a swarm of quarks and leptons that we add labels to.

You can take a pile and swap one grain for another. The pile hasn't changed. A mind can (and does!) replace old thoughts with new ones the same way.

"I am my thoughts" is false, given that your thoughts change every day.

Perhaps we are that which changes our thoughts.

Or maybe we're a cloud of sensations that feels like a self.

Once you understand this on a gut level, changing your thoughts becomes easy. Why should a pile care if a grain is removed? How simple is it to add a new one?

This isn't about learning to let go of old ideas. It's accepting that there's nothing that could hold onto them in the first place.

If you want an exercise that can help you, I'm happy to oblige:

Earlier today I meditated by focusing on a single sense - in this case, the sound of water trickling along a creek.

I placed all of my attention here.

I thought about how the sound of water exists as vibrations in the air. On another level, the sound only existed in my brain - a reconstruction of electrical impulses from my ears.

The part of my brain that thinks of 'me' as a person relaxed. The separation between 'me' and the environment weakened.

It felt as though the sound were a part of me, as much as I think my hands are.

Then it continued.

I thought of myself as being the sound of the water, while that body over there was part of the environment.

It only lasted a moment, but the relief was intense.

People often describe feeling connected to everyone and everything, as if the barriers that separate us come down.

I don't know if that's literally what happens.

All I know is it's a healthy and wonderful thing to experience.

When your mind is this open, there's nothing more natural than to leave behind ideas that don't help you anymore.

Enlightenment is in the details

People learning to meditate go through a series of phases. It's like anything else, really.

You blunder about for a while. It's hard to say whether you're making any progress. Everything seems strange, awkward, pointless and confusing.

But if you stick with it, you have some small wins. It's more from luck than anything, but it gives you a taste for what meditation is like.

Or rather, what you think it's like. But, hey, it's a step in the right direction.

And every step yields rewards. Hesitantly at first - maybe just enough to keep you going. You feel healthier, more focused and more energetic.

Meditation becomes easier. You have bad days and they are hard to overcome. Between those, though, you become more consistent. On a given day, you can reach a wonderful inner state.

Then your consistency begins to evolve into something else.

Skill.

Mastery.

Power.

The control you have over your own mind accelerates. You become a completely different person. Each improvement frees you up to improve more.

You might plateau as you consolidate your transformation. Then you start improving all over again.

With each period of growth, there's an interesting by-product of your blossoming power. You begin to notice more subtle things. Meditation makes you aware of your own awareness, conscious of your consciousness.

Subtlety is underrated. A fine attention allows you to be aware of things you'd normally be unconscious about.

Then, you learn to articulate them.

This is true mastery. Describing experiences gives you control over them.

When you notice a sensation for the first time, it moves from your unconscious mind to your conscious mind. When you find the words to capture it, you have a choice:

You can enhance it or diminish it.

It's as easy as breathing.

A new meditator might say that "nothing" happens. Then, as they learn, they say it felt relaxing.

Listen to an experienced meditator describe it. If you can find a monk, even better. They talk about different degrees of emptiness, relaxation and tension. Sensations shift and evolve moment to moment, as they realise what they need to do to enhance the experience.

They use so many different words to describe the familiar. It's never just one thing to them because they can see the subtlety. They find nuances within nuances, describing what a novice would fail to notice.

This is the next thing to aspire for. Pay attention to the details. Notice what used to escape you. Mark each as a milestone in your progress.

How You Breathe is How You Do Everything

One of the best meditation exercises is to pay attention to your breathing. It's something that most people ignore, which gives you lots of room to improve. It's simple to understand and challenging to master.

And it really opens up the benefits to you.

At first, it's little more than a handy stream of sensations for you to anchor your attention.

Then it becomes something else.

Your breath is never the same at any two points in the cycle. And no two cycles are the same.

When you focus and see that level of detail – where your very breathing becomes interesting – your mind grows stronger.

This is true of any other sensation. If you paid attention to your right thumb, you would notice the same thing.

Your breathing does something, though, that your thumb will never do.

It brings air into your body and expels toxins.

(Cue sounds of shock and outrage.)

Your nose is not some humble valve, though. It's not like a helium tank that, once spun, fills balloons.

Nothing in your body is ever that simple.

Instead, your breathing is a complex mesh of control, sensation and feedback loops. How you breathe influences how you do everything else.

If breathing were a simple intake of oxygen, then breathing faster would be better. As long as you weren't stressing your lungs, getting more air is better than getting less.

Right?

Think of someone who's breathing rapidly and you're not thinking of someone in their moment of power.

Of course, that's a judgement, something you might want to avoid. It's good practice to simply observe your breathing without any desire to alter it.

At first, at least.

Once you're comfortable holding your attention in a calm, accepting way, then you can start to change your breathing.

To relax and balance your body and mind, breathe in a relaxed and balanced way. Aim to extend each breath, slowly at first. Keep the inhalation and exhalation the same length and rate.

If you want a number to aim for, try five or six seconds to inhale, then the same to exhale. That sounds easier than it is for most people. Build up to that slowly. If you need a week or two, take the time. The goal is not to stress your system.

Like life, you can take things slow, steady and balanced.

And if you want more energy and focus?

Then slowly inhale through the nose. To exhale, release your breath through the mouth all at once. Repeat.

And hold your attention in the usual way.

Breathe and Look Ridiculous

You can breathe in a steady, gentle, slow and balanced way. When each inhale is the same length as your exhale, your breath can be a continuous flow. This balance is nothing compared to the balance you'll experience in your mind.

Symmetry isn't everything, though. If you slowly inhale to build up pressure, then release it through your mouth in one, quick burst, you'll notice it energising you like a warm cup of coffee.

People might look at you strangely. That's okay, because looking ridiculous is good training.

So how ridiculous can you look by breathing?

If you like to think in pictures, you might see each style of breathing as a different shape. One is a sine wave; the other, a punctured balloon.

Different patterns for different outcomes.

And so you might wonder: what other shapes can your breathing take?

Well, there's triangular breathing.

Once you can breathe around five times a minute without straining yourself, the next step is to introduce pauses. This can distract you during your meditation or enhance the experience. Experiment and see what happens.

You can inhale, then hold the breath, then exhale, all for equal counts. When you can do this naturally, this breathing pattern centres you. In fact, they teach it in Systema – the martial art developed by Russian special forces.

The next progression is to invert that triangle. Inhale, then exhale, then hold the breath.

I have to remind you of safety. Take care when changing your breathing, especially with this last one. Make your changes slowly and build up over weeks. If you feel discomfort, then breathe normally.

Once you can comfortably follow both triangular patterns, you can combine them into square breathing. You hold twice per cycle – after inhaling and after exhaling.

When you can breathe like this without it distracting you, it changes your body and mind. This isn't necessary for deep meditation...

... but you might find it helps.

There's one more shape to mention. This humble breathing exercise is easier than those I just mentioned. It feels like someone is scrubbing your insides clean with each cycle.

Even if it does make you look a bit ridiculous.

Ignore that impulse if it arises. It's a judgement and a distraction.

The technique of Nadi Shodhana involves inhaling through your right nostril, then exhaling through your left. Then you inhale through the left and exhale through the right.

The best way to do this is to block the unused nostril with your finger. (On the outside, people – this is not an excuse to pick your nose...)

How does this work?

I don't know. Does it matter? See for yourself that it works, then worry about why it does.

Think Meditation is Torture? You Might be Right

If you're unlucky enough to be an Iranian dissident, you probably know about white torture. Also known as sensory deprivation, it's a nasty piece of work.

You don't have to cause pain to break someone. All you need are blacked out goggles, noise cancelling headphones and time. Lots of time.

The brain is excellent at extrapolating meaning from snippets of data. A few dimples on bright red flesh makes you think "strawberry". Two dots and a curve look like a happy face. A brief odour conjures memories, emotions and actions.

But when there's no data to find meaning in...

Well, that part of you is still active. It still looks for the meaning in data that isn't there.

Your brain craves novelty, interaction and stimulus. Strip that away and it's like turning the brain against itself.

You don't get used to it. Time only makes it worse.

I wouldn't wish it in my worst enemy, assuming I had one.

I would recommend it as a meditation technique though.

In small doses, sensory deprivation is a valuable tool for probing your psyche. It's calming to be away from all that noise and distraction. What makes it pleasant, as opposed to torture, is that you can walk away from it. Stimulation and deprivation in a continual cycle.

You can experience this by renting a flotation tank for an hour or so. You float in a saline solution, with no sound and nothing to see. It's incredibly centring. If you want to try it on your own, all you need is an eye mask, headphones and some white noise. YouTube has plenty of tracks.

Set aside some time, close off the world and go inside.

What this does is interesting. I mentioned your brain's instinct is to extract meaning from small signals. I also mentioned that this keeps happening, even when during sensory deprivation.

The experience is just like dreaming. Random images flash before your eyes. Your brain does the best it can with what few signals arrive. Is that a squirrel or a fireplace? What colour is that... bicycle?

But as soon as it has an image, it discards it and tries something else.

I was surprised by how quick and intense these hallucinations were. I think it only took a few minutes before it immersed me completely. Then again, it's hard to measure time in this state.

This might be one of the easiest meditation techniques, but I don't recommend it for beginners. After all, you're playing with fire here. It's safe enough for most people - having said that, knowing how to control your experience helps.

I see why people use white noise to fall asleep though. Once I started dreaming, it was hard to stay awake.

Appendix A: Types of Meditation

Ancient, Trendy Ideas

It's interesting when something that's thousands of years old becomes trendy. What relevance do ancient teachings have today?

If the teachings endure on their own merits, then they're timeless. They must contain some element of truth that appeals to people. Continents and millennia don't dull the spark of a truly useful idea.

Speaking of ancient and popular ideas, have you heard about mindfulness?

Mindfulness is one of those ideas that sounds too simple to work. It involves bringing your attention, without judgement, into the present moment.

Big deal, right? Don't people do that already?

Well... if you've spent much time meditating, you know the answer to that.

One of the great powers of the mind is casting itself back through memories or projections of the future. You can think of the past and plan for what comes next. These thoughts are so vivid that they can pull you in. You lose yourself in your memories and imagination as hours roll by.

This isn't a bad thing. Learning from the past and anticipating the future are useful, even essential. But if mindfulness involves focusing on the present moment, then why is it so beneficial?

The problem doesn't come from thinking of other times.

It comes from dwelling on them.

If something traumatic happens, some people fixate on it for decades to come. They think back on it in their quiet moments.

This is natural. The brain wants to learn as much as it can from dramatic events. Knowing what happened can prevent it from happening again.

The problem is that it comes at a cost... one that grows steeper over time. The first hour of reflecting teaches you a lot. So does the second. A year or ten from then, though, you aren't learning much. All you're doing is reactivating the emotions surrounding the experience.

You train yourself to feel a certain way through repetition. The more you can focus on the positive, instead, the better you'll be.

Does that mean that dwelling on happy memories is okay? In small doses, sure - reliving a pleasant event is fantastic exercise for the mind. But, again, there are diminishing returns. Have you ever thought of a good memory you'd forgotten about? The emotional rush can be intense. When you think of it an hour later, the glow is a little bit weaker. Eventually, that reward becomes not worth the cost.

When you think of the future, you're either worrying or fantasising. The same rules apply as with remembering. If you think about a great future, it inspires and elevates you.

The problem with remembering and imagining is that you pay a price. You think of other times at the expense of now. The present moment is the only thing you can control and take action. The past is gone and the future isn't here yet, but now is present.

There are many things happening in the moment. The world buzzes with sensory experiences, so experience them. If you cast your mind away, then you miss what's happening now. And, since your mind constructs memories and imagination, what happens now is the only thing that's real.

This is the value of mindfulness. It grounds you in reality. When you choose to think of other times, you maintain yourself through the experience.

Unreal emotions can't seduce you away from your moment of power.

This is what makes mindfulness and meditation such a potent combination. When you learn to open up to the experiences of the moment, it teaches you to think and be in new ways.

The Harry Potter School of Meditation

There's a style of meditation that could have come right from the pages of fantasy.

It's the closest thing we Muggles have to magic.

And, in the world beyond Diagon Alley, it's the fuel for the most powerful magic there is.

It keeps people safe from things that should harm them. It even blocks unblockable spells - the ultimate power.

I am, of course, talking about love.

But not just any love. After all, that's an emotion felt across the human species. If all a wizard needed was to feel something, everyone could use it.

Yet in the books, love-based magic is ancient and mysterious.

Intriguing, isn't it?

And what does this have to do with meditation?

There's a style of meditation called metta, also known as loving-kindness meditation. As the name suggests, you reflect on love. Not greedy love or possessive love, but kind love.

It's a wholesome and pure emotion.

Most people feel this at times. There are those in your life who invoke something deeper than infatuation or admiration. We call these people our soulmates or brother/sister. And, because we know the words can't convey it, we inject so much energy into the label.

There are "brothers" and then there are *brothers*.

You can practice this state of mind. Like any other thought, it gets stronger with time and attention.

It's easy to start with the people who inspire you to feel this way about them.

Then you move onto people who know but don't think about much. When you practice loving-kindness towards them, it frees you from the barriers you erect towards other people.

Once you can do that, you practice with strangers. Think of unknown people in distant lands who you'll never meet. When you experience loving-kindness for a person who's as much an idea as reality, it opens you up even more.

Then, the final stage. Feeling love and kindness to your enemies. Genuinely wishing people well, even those who have done you wrong.

Now, some people get offended by this idea. There are people who have done horrible, unforgiveable things. They think that to wish love and kindness on them downplays every wrong thing they did.

Except, I assure you, it doesn't.

This isn't about saying that what they did was okay. It isn't about welcoming cruel and evil people back into your life.

You forgive them for you, not for them. If they are the sort of people who would exploit that, then you can never let them know. Wish them love and kindness in the privacy of your thoughts.

This makes you strong.

Impossibly strong.

Because when you can forgive someone even as you cut them from your life, it releases their power over you.

It makes you impervious to the little things that other people can do. Would you even notice a moment of rudeness from a stranger if you're capable of this much compassion?

A weak person curses their enemies. A strong person never wastes a thought or emotion on them ever again.

If You Can't Quiet Your Mind, Louden It

I hear so, so many people say they "can't" meditate. And it's usually for similar reasons.

They say they can't concentrate or quiet their thinking. They think they can't sit still long enough.

If you've ever said or thought anything like this, I politely invite you to snap out of it.

First of all, I've never played golf before. If I picked up a club tomorrow and went madly swinging across a course, I'd be terrible.

If I wanted to boost my skills and lower my scores, what would I need to do? Practice, of course. Intelligent practice, probably with some coaching, over months or years.

Meditation is the same way, only with an extra wrinkle. If I've never played golf, I have the advantage of starting from nothing. You've been thinking your entire life, though. You have to unlearn more than you need to learn.

You might need more time and more intelligent practice before you see results.

Which brings me to my second point:

Who says you need to quiet your mind?

Meditation involves focusing on a single thing in the here and now. Often that means you need to quiet your mind.

Or you can make your thoughts louder and focus on those.

In fact, you could think a single thought. You could make it so loud that it drowns out everything else. There's no room for effort or distractions.

Why not? Once you understand the principles of meditation, this solution becomes obvious.

But if you are going to think a single thought, you should probably make it a good one.

This is where a mantra becomes useful.

A mantra is a word or phrase that is more than just a word or phrase. It captures everything you are and wish you could be. It speaks to your ideal self and tempts them into being.

Your mantra can begin with "I am…" or "I will be…"

And it should tell anyone you choose to share it with everything about you.

What is it you truly desire? Who is it that you really are? What are you becoming?

Take some time to get your mantra right. This single thought will occupy your attention, so it pays to craft it well. That said, it doesn't need to be perfect to begin. Find something that resonates with you and keep exploring.

You have outgrown many things - clothes, toys, hobbies. You can outgrow mantras, too. But only if you begin.

The Most Ancient Meditation Practice on Earth

Buddhism is about 2,500 years old. It's an oppressive amount of time. A hundred generations (give or take) have lived, shaped the world and died during that span. No empires and few cities have survived since then.

Looking back in time a fifth of the way there brings you to Leonardo da Vinci's day. Going back halfway puts you in Charlemagne's Holy Roman Empire.

It is an old style of meditation.

But it's not the oldest.

There's a school of meditation that's still alive today. It stretches back much, much further.

Forget 2,500 years - we're talking tens of thousands of years. It might be as old as the culture that created it, which goes back 40,000 years.

If not more.

It comes from the people native to the Daly River region in the Northern Territory of Australia. They call this practice *dadirri* and it is breathtaking.

The Aboriginal people describe it as having a silent awareness. Meditators sit for hours among nature, listening to the wind and water.

You might think this sounds like mindfulness. It is mindfulness, with a twist.

Buddhism teaches you to be present with the experience. Whatever your senses detect is for you to process with your full attention. No distractions, no judgements, until you lose yourself in your awareness of now.

Dadirri teaches you to listen to nature. Experience the senses - again, without distraction or judgement - with silence and full appreciation.

It's a subtle distinction, but an important one. Listening in this way is active and interactive. You don't just observe nature. Instead, you learn everything you can from her.

Meditation improves your problem-solving abilities, even more than simply thinking about the challenge. Why? Because meditation opens your mind to new patterns of thought. If the solution doesn't lie in your conscious mind, then it must lie in your unconscious.

I haven't seen any studies on this, but my guess would be that dadirri beats regular mindfulness.

When your mind is open and you pay attention, you realise that nature can teach you a lot about your solution. The wind, rain, rivers and earth hold your answers.

Do I mean that literally? Or am I speaking metaphorically and that spending time in nature inspires you?

It doesn't matter. Just know that if this idea sounds like fuzzy hippy nonsense, then you need to go deeper in your meditation trances. Your brain won't speak to you in words but in metaphors. If you need determination like a river, flexibility like the wind, intensity like the sun or stability like the earth, then that's how it'll speak to you.

And if you don't get an answer, all you'll have done is reconnected to nature deeper than you have in your life. That alone makes it worth learning.

Appendix B: Meditation and Religion

If You Enjoy Freedom, Then Meditate

What role does meditation play in Buddhism?

That might seem like a strange question. It plays an important role, certainly. It's one of the key pillars of the faith.

But what, exactly, does it do?

In Christianity, the purpose of prayer is to connect you with God. Some see it as literally talking to Him, while others see it as opening yourself up to receive what He has to offer.

There are elements of this in Buddhism, sure.

It's also completely different.

Meditation is nothing short than the pursuit of freedom. I'm writing this a couple of days before the United States celebrates the 4th of July, so maybe freedom is on my mind. I stand by it, though. The practice offers nothing short of total liberation.

Freedom and liberation from what, though?

The world holds many temptations, lures and distractions. These aren't all bad things. For an altruist, helping people in need is deeply rewarding.

Virtue is a vice when it's something you can't ignore.

Then there are the real distractions – what most people think of as vices. People chase these things, even if getting them won't help them.

Think of someone desperate for a promotion so they can move from a suburban box to a larger suburban box. This goal might consume years of hard work and frustration. As soon as they get it, they feel unsatisfied. They start looking for the next bigger box to acquire.

Ambition and commerce have their place. Things go awry when people believe that they'll be happy once they reach the next milestone.

They work for years to build themselves a prison.

Maybe you don't own a house. That doesn't make you free if your prison is made of other pursuits.

For some, they must keep up with the latest fashions.

Others buy gadgets they don't want or need.

Still others drudge for 11.5 months of the year to afford a brief holiday.

If these are what give life meaning, they'll always feel less than fulfilled.

There's always something new to chase. So what would happen if they stopped chasing? What if, for a moment, they ripped their eyes away from the distant horizon and looked around them?

The moment they find themselves in the moment, they begin to feel free. This might be for the first time in their lives.

What happens next is up to them. Maybe they'll still pursue the promotion, only this time they do it with both eyes open. They don't defer satisfaction to some future event outside their control. They seize their attention and bring it to the present.

In a world where everyone looks forward or back, being present is true freedom.

Where Meditation is Controversial

Anyone who knows me knows that I am in favour of meditation. I think it's wonderful. Is it for everyone? Maybe, maybe not – but this is low hanging fruit for the human race. If most people invested a little bit more into the practice, the results would more than pay for the time.

Not everyone agrees that meditation is worthwhile, though.

There are people who think it doesn't do anything.

(The science is emphatically against them on this one.)

Then there are those who see it as a bad thing.

(Again, science wants to give them a stern talking to.)

No communities demonstrate the range better than the Abrahamic faiths.

Most people in these religions get it. A lot of them use 'prayer' and 'meditation' interchangeably, and so they should. Both involve closing your eyes to the world and opening your mind to something greater.

Deep prayer has excellent odds of putting you in a meditative trance. If something outside of yourself wanted to reach you, doing that while you're in this state is the best way. You're more likely to hear and act on new ideas.

On the other hand, there are quite a few readers accusing me of blasphemy right now.

There are people – religious or not – who think meditation weakens your mental health. They say that exploring your mind invites savage behaviour, psychosis and nervous breakdowns.

Or demons.

It's a strange idea and I think I know where it comes from.

One root of this belief is good old-fashioned racism. In the height of the 'yellow peril' days, Eastern religions were considered devil worship.

We've come a long way since then. Asian culture used to be as exotic as you could find. Now, it's becoming more familiar and mainstream each day.

But some ideas linger.

It isn't all xenophobia, though.

I also blame Freud.

Freud viewed the subconscious as a dark, evil, hostile place. It was a mental realm of suppressed violence, depravity and barbarism.

There's a reason why I don't use his word for it. The unconscious mind is more than our animal impulses. It houses our instincts and intuitions. It's where our visions of our greatest selves live. This part of you guides you to what you want and shields you from harm.

How Freud thought that everything good came from the conscious mind is beyond me.

But he had enough good ideas to influence modern psychology. Part of his legacy is tainting anything that brings unconscious material into your awareness.

Meditation brings you in touch with your angels. It teaches you how to overcome your demons. That's what prayer does for you, which is no coincidence. Both practices are, at their heart, the same.

A Different Style of Leadership, Living and Learning

Shamanism is a broad term. It describes religions from Australia to America and everywhere in between. These religions are incredibly diverse, each with its own unique rituals and cultural elements.

They have a lot in common, too. The spiritual leaders have deep connections to nature, their community and themselves.

These people live off the land without much technology. If they have a problem, they need to solve it. They need to make sense of a vast, confusing and challenging world.

It takes a lot of strength to survive without civilisation. Having technology - whether that's spears or something more advanced - isn't enough. Being able to communicate, strategise and plan isn't enough.

You need to learn to think like nature.

Animals act on instincts. This gives them the advantage of always having a plan. These instincts tend to work, otherwise they'd be expunged from the gene pool. They are quick, effective and reliable.

Human-level intelligence may be slow and costly. It takes decades for a baby to become an adult. There's always the risk that they'll learn the wrong thing.

But it does have one major advantage.

It allows you to steal the best instincts from the animal kingdom (and develop new ones).

There's a quirk with humans where we grow our minds through our clothing. We civilised folk are not above this instinct. This is why young kinds sneak into their parents' wardrobes and play dress up. It's why people feel more confident in a business suit, military uniform or lab coat. Clothes reflect our psyches, and vice versa.

Shamans take this to the next level. They wear costumes of predators and prey. Then they work themselves into a frenzied altered state. In this state, the boundaries between skin and clothing melt.

They learn to think like the animal they wear.

If you think I'm exaggerating, then I have good news: you have so much more to gain from meditation. If you've never seen the world from a wolf's perspective - or even a tree's or a cloud's - then you have more to learn.

Shamans use meditation to tap into their own power. They need the flexibility to see the correct course of action. They need the charisma to lead the people through hard times. When disaster strikes, they need to provide the way forwards.

When I talk about mind training, this is the model I have in mind. It's not just about releasing anxiety. It's about peering into the jungle - concrete or otherwise - and seeing the patterns, hum and rhythms of nature.

Appendix C: Meditation and Humanism

The Rewards for Living Ethically

Where does morality come from?

Some people point outside themselves. It comes from a divine creator, they say. Others say that you can calculate and quantify morality from the laws of physics.

I'm not sure about those. Maybe morality is a gift we receive from elsewhere. My theory on its origins is much simpler.

If you were to compare two people in our evolutionary pre-history – one who was ethical, one who was not – you'd notice the answer.

Someone without any morality would steal food when they were hungry. They'd murder their rivals over petty squabbles. They would undermine the group's politics for any advantage.

If you think someone like this would outcompete an altruist, you're wrong. It takes a community to survive the wilderness. Exile was a punishment practically equivalent to execution.

In other words, if people don't like you, you're doomed.

If you're a threat to your own tribe, that's even worse.

Play by the tribe's rules or pay the price.

Ethical behaviour seems to be a legacy of our biology. We have an innate sense that some things are good and others are bad. Our emotions reward us with virtuous pride or punish with anxious guilt.

A perfect system, right...?

Well, obviously not. Have a look around and you won't see a utopia.

Knowing that some behaviours are good is one thing. That's innate for most of us. Learning what those behaviours are comes from our upbringing.

There's a great line from the Carl Jung book, Modern Man in Search of a Soul. A tribal chieftain was asked what the difference between good and bad is. He said something like:

"Good is when I steal my enemy's wives. Bad is when he steals mine."

What does that sound like? Greed? Hypocrisy?

Or perhaps that's a useful way of viewing the world when you have to fight for survival.

Some people honestly see having children as immoral. Most of us would, I hope, see 'stealing wives' as immoral (on a few levels). Biology creates a sense of ethics within us, but what is moral is something we learn.

It's not arbitrary, but it's close.

The other problem with morality is that people can ignore it.

"I know stealing is wrong... but I really want that new phone. The corporation who made it is rich and greedy – they won't miss it. I donate money to charity and this will help me earn more, so it's a net win."

And on and on the justifications flow.

Unless, of course, you're in tune with your unconscious mind.

I surprise people when I tell them that being in a hypnotic trance makes you more ethical. Some people have this notion that you could be hypnotised into, say, robbing a bank. Outside of a trance, you can justify robbing a bank as easily as you can justify stealing a phone.

You can't lie to yourself inside of a trance.

Meditation creates the same conditions.

Whatever form your conscious takes, you hear it more clearly when you go inside your mind.

And when your conscious knows you're listening, it stops fighting you. Which means every part of your mind aligns with your intention.

Good behaviour has its rewards.

You Are a Limitless Frontier

Exploration captivates the human psyche. There's something noble about wandering off into uncharted, untamed land. Many people would risk their lives to be the first to see a new island, a new planet, a new sun in the sky.

Our ancestors were explorers. The ones who preferred to stay put limited themselves to what they had. Their cousins with wanderlust inherited the rest of the Earth.

There's that saying about how we're born too late to explore the Earth and too soon to explore the galaxy.

I wonder if that's true. The Earth still has uncharted territories. Even if we map the surface, that leaves the ocean floor. And under the surface, too.

Also, who says that we won't get to see the galaxy? Maybe we're the first folk to live forever. Maybe cheap faster-than-light travel is a decade away.

In any case, it doesn't matter. If you have the urge to explore, then you have options.

The first is to find some corner of the world that's new to you. It's still exploration, even if others have seen it before.

The second is to turn your horizon-hungry eyes inwards. You have a rich, unexplored universe floating between your ears.

You might think you know what goes on inside your mind. I promise that there's always more to explore.

If the surface of the Earth (including oceans) represented your mind, how much of that is what you already consciously experience?

Is it about a hemisphere?

A continent?

A country?

Maybe a city?

Well, I had fun finding some numbers. If we take the research of a scientist called Nørretranders, we get some interesting comparisons.

If a map of the Earth is our mind, then our consciousness is about:

- 6% the size of Belgium,
- one and a half times the size of Sydney,
- five times the size of the Isle of Wight,
- half the size of Yosemite National Park.

(Assuming my calculations are correct. I was working with some strange numbers here.)

And that's very generous in favour of consciousness. Modern research casts doubt on Nørretranders' numbers - what you're aware of is probably only a fraction of that. But let's take it as a given.

Imagine having an entire planet to explore, but only spending time in one large city. You could live a full life there. There's enough for you to grow up, work, study, learn, fall in and out of love, and go on wild adventures in this city.

Then imagine if you left.

What if you chartered a plane and just left. You took off to chase the horizon, only returning when you wanted to.

No one could ever see it all. You might find a favourite shoreline and spend your time exploring that, or you could always be on the move. Either way, you'd never run out of things to learn.

This world inside of you is vast. Like the Earth, it's finite but beyond any human's lifetime. And, like the Earth, it holds treasures beyond what the first explorers could imagine.

Mundane Magic and Scientific Sorcery

Neurons do something strange when starved of oxygen. First, they start firing randomly. Then they start to shut down. If they don't receive precious oh-two soon, they start to die.

This sequence is, of course, an oversimplification. You'll find counter examples all over the place.

Even so, this sequence explains a lot.

When certain parts of the brain (the temporal lobe and a few others) start misfiring, you receive a flood of memories. This can vary from an unusual montage of random events to full-blown hallucinations.

When the whole brain starts firing randomly, that's a seizure. But when parts of it spark off for no reason, it can create predictable effects. For example, in the occipital lobe, this can lead to seeing a spinning vortex of light. It's dark around the edges, probably because peripheral vision shuts down first.

Even your sense of balance can do weird things. The misfires followed by a shutdown can create the sense that every direction is the same.

And if the left brain weakens first (or the right brain starts misfiring more intensely), then you receive an incredible sense of peace, knowledge and connection to the universe. Even as your consciousness fades.

When conditions are right, you get a sense of floating, hallucinations, your life flashing before your eyes and the 'light-at-the-end-of-the-tunnel' effect.

And there you have it: a plausible, mundane explanation for near death experiences.

Is this model accurate?

I don't know.

It's probably missing a few details.

But, if it's in the right direction, it explains one of the most spiritual experiences people have without assuming that humans have souls. This works, even if we are no more than squishy meat computers.

Don't think I'm doing this because I'm a cruel, mirthless stereotype of a rationalist. The moral is not that, having explained it, the experience is meaningless.

No - the moral is that our brains are incredible.

If you want to experience any of those effects, you don't need to almost die on a surgeon's table. The brain can create any of those experiences at any time.

Sure, it requires a lot of mind training to reach that point. And, yes, some are easier to achieve than others are.

But I've achieved most of them. I've had a few out-of-body experiences, most of them accidental. There were times when it felt like I floated around the room or down the street. I've talked to dead people (and fictitious people).

And I've felt the sublime joy that comes from being connected to the universe.

You don't need a soul, spirit, aura or any kind of disembodied energy shadow to do this. Your unconscious mind has incredible powers. As a child, you learn to suppress these experiences. It's a part of growing up and seeing what's real as opposed to what's "just" in your head.

Things in your head still have value, though. Every invention once existed as only a hallucination. Every metre of social progress was once a dream.

Your choice in life is not between embracing religion and living a dull, materialistic existence. There is magic in the mundane and sorcery in the science. Even bound by the laws of physics, the universe is amazing.

You are amazing.

Made in the USA
Columbia, SC
01 December 2018